A Backward Child

The Remembrances of Architect William Dew

by William Dew

E.M. Productions
Warrenton, VA

A BACKWARD CHILD: *The Remembrances of Architect William Dew*

E.M. Productions
P.O. Box 336
Warrenton, VA 20188

Library of Congress Cataloging-in-Publication Data

Dew, William (William Bland), 1908-
A backward child : the remembrances of architect William Dew / by William Dew.
p. cm.
ISBN 1-880664-40-2 (alk. paper)
1. Dew, William (William Bland), 1908- 2. Architects--Virginia--Biography. I. Title.

NA737.D49A2 2003
720'.92--dc22
[B]

2003064266

ACKNOWLEDGMENT

Billy Dew arrived in Middleburg four years before I was born and fifty-six years before I became Mayor. By the time I was old enough to understand and appreciate all that was special about my hometown, it had become yet more special with the construction of the Community Center, the new Middleburg Bank building and other significant Main Street projects that were the product of Billy's architectural genius.

The Community Center will, I believe, prove to be Billy's most enduring and important contribution to the town. It was a particular honor for me to be part of the Center's 50th anniversary celebration in its elegant main ballroom—an event that featured and feted Billy. Judging from the broad smiles he bore and the stories he spun that day (including his telling of the debate whether the main room should be a basketball court rather than a ballroom—a debate that interrupted construction and delayed completion of either) I think that Billy was especially proud of that particular building as well.

Billy's life was, of course, bigger than Middleburg, as he recounts here. But for me, Billy was Middleburg and Middleburg was Billy. It was always striking to me that a man of such humble bearing produced buildings that were, in a quiet and inconspicuous way, elegant and majestic.

But then again, it all made sense. Billy was not burdened by an ego that drove him to design structures that "made a statement." He came to Middleburg, absorbed the history and character of the community and produced buildings that echoed and enhanced the best of what was here already.

But Billy's buildings are more than simply pleasing architecture; they are active, vital working parts of the town. The Community Center quickly became and remains today exactly what its name denotes—a center for activities— swimming, baseball, volleyball, (sorry, no basketball) picnics, dances, bowling, meetings, fireworks, dog shows, flower shows, craft shows—you name it; it's been at the Community Center and will probably be back. It seems in fact that all of Billy's buildings—from the Bank to the ABC Store—are heavily trafficked by one constituency or another.

It was our good fortune that Billy chose Middleburg as his home. His creative talent has added both grace and function to the community. He will be remembered fondly by those who knew him; his buildings will be admired and enjoyed by all who make this their destination for generations to come.

Tim Dimos
Mayor, Middleburg

EDITOR'S NOTE

Mr. William B. Dew, Jr., came to me with his manuscript, *A Backward Child*, in 1999. I was delighted to meet this legendary architect, and I was taken with his somewhat fictionalized tale of his life. We discussed the need to rewrite a number of passages and some entire chapters. Mr. Dew was willing, and though the years had slowed him a bit, he commenced work immediately.

At the time of Mr. Dew's death in 2000, we were still editing the book you now hold in your hands. The final chapter was in heavy rewrite. The entire photographic insert was in the planning stage. Mr. Dew had selected a number of photographs and drawings for inclusion; sad to say, many of these visuals have been lost since his death. What remains for you to read and view is our best effort at capturing the essence of *A Backward Child*. The staff of E.M. Productions worked to validate time and place where possible and where necessary. We foraged for photographs and other visuals to include in the insert; we believe we have succeeded in bringing you a profile of this beloved, talented man.

As Mr. Dew's editor, I came to know him well. He and I had some rather heated discussions regarding revisions to his cherished manuscript. I can only hope I have done it justice now that it is in its finished form. I must say that I consider it a privilege to have known and worked with such a gentleman.

Beth A. Miller, Publisher and Editor
E.M. Productions

CHAPTER 1

The scene was idyllic: a well designed, new young ladies' college, on thousands of acres of pristine land, with small mountains, virgin forests, and a placid lake. Near the center of this best-of-all-worlds was an expansive garden, beautifully designed, perfectly maintained, with enormous boxwood bushes, old trees, and flowering shrubs. Facing a spacious boxwood circle was a substantial century-and-a-half-old manor house. Built in the romantic period of architecture, it had well proportioned, wide, but not high, towers and an arch-over-arch portico centered between them.

It befell on this day that, within the manor house, the new members of the board of directors of the future college had come to order. The initial speeches, erudite and smooth, as might have been expected from the board members of a new college, finally got around to the main point of the day: selecting a business manager and treasurer for the college.

The chairman, Clayton Manson, proposed his brother-in-law, William Bland Dew. "He comes from a fine old family from Tidewater. His great-great-uncle was president of William and Mary University. He does not drink, is a person of high Victorian morality, is happily married, steady going, and highly reliable. For more than a century his family owned one of the premier plantations in their part of Tidewater. In addition, his wife, Natalie, comes from a popular and highly respectable large, old land-owning family from right across the river. Adding all this up, I believe we could not do better." Then he added, thoughtfully, "The point has been made that the Dews would have a problem with their children. There is no school anywhere nearby except Amherst, the poorest school in the state, and to get to it one would have to ride the horse-drawn school wagon—a very long process. Otherwise the place might be ideal for children: intellectual stimulation, ten thousand acres to play in, the lake to swim and fish in, and, perhaps later, horses to ride."

When the meeting was over, their kind secretary said, in leaving the room, "The children, Billy and Polly Cary, are going to have problems."

And so they did.

One fine Sunday afternoon several years later, William Dew and his friend, who was an Episcopal minister, were returning from a rather long walk around the lake and up to the "Monument," the old cemetery of the original owners of the plantation. It was a pretty place where one could see for miles in every direction. The two men were talking seriously about the children. "William, the children will have a wonderful place to grow up in: half a county to roam around in, a nice little chapel right here at the college, probably religious school every week. Perhaps they could take art or music classes right here, and we hope the college minister will give them religious instruction. There is no other school except at Amherst, but the Lord will provide. They are nice children, and they are going to be just fine, William."

William replied, "Tom, I am so glad you said that. Naturally, I am worried, but Natalie is going to have a little school. There are two or three faculty children, and she will tutor them all. The only trouble is little Billy will be the only boy and he's the youngest child. Natalie is afraid he will be terribly lonesome. In fact, she has invited a relative, Tom Torrey, from Lynchburg for this weekend to keep him company. We will bring them up in the church and I feel everything will be all right.

"But Natalie is very worried about little Billy; she thinks he may grow up to be terribly reclusive. I do not agree. People are born to either be good mixers or not to be. Anyhow, they will not learn to curse and speak vulgarities as the children do now."

"Well spoken, William," replied the minister. "And we will say our prayers for them."

They were now coming in sight of William's home. Natalie was waiting for them on the porch. She calmly said, "Don't let this upset you, but we have had a problem. The children were playing inside the house. Polly Cary, as usual, was more or less bossing everyone. No one would do as Billy wanted, so he went outside, got a rock, came in, and threw it at his sister and chipped her tooth."

"How on earth did this happen?" inquired William.

"Billy wanted to go down and wade in the brook. No, that wouldn't do; Polly Cary wanted to go in the house and use the toy cook stove. Tom went with her. Billy, furious, followed, angrily shouting that they wouldn't do anything he wanted. Polly Cary closed the door and wouldn't let him in. Billy went outside, picked up a rock and came in the back door. He then called Polly Cary out into the hall, threw the rock and hit her in the mouth."

Natalie then added, somewhat wistfully, "I know you

believe in spare the rod and spoil the child, but Billy has thought it over and feels awfully bad about it."

Indeed he had. He was practically trembling, he was so afraid of his father. "Father, please give me a spanking."

William walked around the house a few minutes to consider the matter, then came back and said, "Billy, I know you didn't mean to do it. We will just forget about it."

This was during the summer recess. The college and most of its parts were closed. Most of the faculty members had left, but those remaining, including the Dews, were enjoying gathering together for their meals in a small faculty dining room. This group, one morning, was expected to include Miss McVeigh, the new president. Those who had not yet met her were waiting in great expectation. This particular morning she was late arriving.

At the dining room entrance, there was a screen door, which had an unusual latch. As the president finally neared, there was a hush in the room. She reached the screen door, but could not work the latch. For a moment, everyone stared blankly. Then, Polly Cary, with no prodding from anyone, got up, walked nicely to the door and opened it for the president.

Miss McVeigh, who was single and childless, was impressed, as were many members of the faculty, who were also single and childless. "That is the prettiest little girl," someone said. This opinion seemed to be shared by all.

"And did you watch the little concert she gave after dinner last night? She was so pretty and played the violin quite well." Polly Cary was often admired, bringing her parents much pleasure.

Natalie Dew was born Natalie Manson at Pebbleton, where her family had lived since the eighteenth century. She was one of three girls. Her sisters married well, the latter becoming Mrs. Robert Massie and the former, Mrs. John Katz.

Mr. Massie, Mattie's husband, was also from an old plantation in Nelson County, and a prominent family. He was strong in the stone and lumber business, among other things. He was Chairman of the Board of V.M.I. He was also quite prominent in the Society of the Cincinnatty, and head of the Virginia Chapter. His family, in the eighteenth-century, had lived in Northern Virginia, but had left saying, "We don't want our children to grow up cock fighters and fox hunters." He still owned a large track of land near Chillicothie, Ohio, which was given to his family by the government at the end of the Revolution.

John Katz's family lived in Bremen, Germany, and were extremely prominent there. John, Sally's husband, had built a tobacco factory in Lynchburg and expected great things from it.

Clayton Manson was Natalie's brother. He, too, was prominent, Lynchburg's leading lawyer, twice its mayor, and Chairman of the Board at Sweet Briar until his death in 1921.

Natalie, the youngest daughter, had had an affair with Guy Langhorne. When it was over, she had entered Randolph Macon College in Lynchburg and later married William Dew. They lived a short while in Wyoming, then came back to Sweet Briar, which was then only becoming established. When Polly Cary was born, she immediately filled an important place in Natalie's affections. They became unusually close.

When Billy was born, Polly Cary was always older, stronger, and much more in their mother's favor. It was almost as if Polly Cary were already grown and a trusted friend of their mother's.

During the summers, some of the college facilities were rented to families from other places who wished to escape the heat, or who simply wished to be out in the country for a time. Some of these families included young children.

One day, Billy, who had learned to build miniature stone walls with pebbles he found in sparse places on the lawn, had built one about two inches high. Some of the larger children wanted to play other games, and one of them destroyed his wall to make a necessary place for them. Billy tried to pick up a rock to defend his wall, but the rock was too heavy and he could only roll it at the other small boy. Fisticuffs ensued. Polly Cary wanted the other games and joined the opponents, making fun of Billy. Their mother heard the commotion and came to quiet it. She, as usual, asked Polly Cary what it was all about. Polly gave Billy's conduct a bad report. Punishment for Billy followed. Worse, he was turned over to his father for a spanking. Then Billy sulked by himself, viewing the other children from a window.

The much older brother of one of the children soon arrived in his family's car. They decided to drive to the lake for a swim. Billy, in the depths of misery, watched them drive away, wishing he could have his freedom.

One afternoon there was a party for the children at the Martindale's home. Billy, tired of the girls, wanted to go fishing with his father. This left no one to walk the half-mile through the woods to the Martindale's home with Polly Cary. Natalie thought this would not do, so no fishing for Billy.

Billy, angry, would not talk to Polly Cary on the way. Coming back, Billy wanted to cut through the woods on a small footpath. Polly Cary wanted to take the longer, but easier road around the woods. Billy started through the

woods and told Polly to follow him. Polly refused and followed the road. Billy, who loved the woods, kept on down
his path. Then he, based on previous experience, began
to sense there would be trouble once they arrived home.
Always ingenious, he thought he might scrape by by shad-
owing Polly Cary, Indian-like, from within the forest.

Previously, William had remarked at the lunch table
about the hired help who worked in the college laundry,
some of whom walked long distances in the early morning
darkness, having laid claim to seeing strange and terrifying
monsters in the woods. The monsters were described as
having big red eyes, and making horrible shrieks and
breathing clouds of smoke. This had appeared very funny
to Billy at the time. However, as Billy was enjoying his cat-
and-mouse game and feeling more like his Indian heroes,
he began to realize the late afternoon was darkening. He
thought he heard something, which he tried to ignore. Then
his whole body stiffened and even his eyes seemed frozen
as he heard a shrill shriek from the treetops and saw large,
bright red eyes.

He was too afraid to move. The eyes were coming down
from the trees toward the ground, obviously coming after
him. Then he heard Polly Cary calling him. She had also
heard the sound and thought she had seen the eyes. She
was scared half to death.

The horrifying shriek came again, and many large
sparks fell to the ground. Then, being a rather bright child,
Billy figured it out. The wind was blowing two large
branches together causing friction, almost igniting them.

Billy joined Polly Cary and, for once, a temporary truce
ensued. Peace was restored. This was fortunate. Friction
was arising over almost everything. The two children hur-
ried home, relieved to be safe once again.

Polly Cary had mastered the art of convincing her mother that everything she wanted was good and necessary. William appeared to his son as stern as the Lord God Jehovah: far away and completely unapproachable. Natalie was full of sympathy, but any matters of discipline were delegated to William. Billy became afraid of his father. He never discussed any problems with him; however, he was still Billy's distant hero.

A split was developing between Natalie and William as to how they should treat their son. William thought Natalie was too sympathetic to the point of spoiling him, and thought more sternness was in order.

His mother's talk of religion turned Billy off. On the way home from church one day, Natalie and Billy passed an improvised table, with, among other things, a small bowl on it for donations to a local charity, in which Natalie placed a crisp new bill. Billy, recalling the minister's sermon on charity, and feeling very grown up at the time, searched in his pocket, brought out a dime, and placed it carefully in the bowl.

Natalie said, "That was nice of you, Billy. I'm sure you feel happy now. That is because you did something good."

This struck Billy the wrong way. He made a mental note never to give to charity again.

One Sunday morning Billy and his father went to the office to get the paper. William opened a drawer, got out a box of Chiclets, and gave one to Billy, who was absolutely thrilled at the unexpected gift. Incidents like this were, however, few and far between.

Natalie and Polly Cary were usually in complete accord. Polly was seldom disciplined in any way. Natalie, perhaps remembering the frustrations of her own childhood, understood Polly Cary's problems. Natalie's own brother, Clayton, was older, and adept at handling his own problems. Natalie did not realize that Billy, being the younger child, not very strong and very much alone, was not that way. For Billy, there was little refuge; there were no other small boys around and his father was preoccupied. There was no one to take his side.

Natalie was extremely religious. She idolized the foreign missionaries. She really thought the church was the most important thing in the country. She was considerate of other people's feelings, even to the extreme. Billy frequently got into disputes with the little girls with whom he had to associate constantly. Natalie would be likely to punish him so as to be sure she was taking a generous course rather than blaming the trouble on the neighbors' children. Polly Cary, being the eldest and the leader, was less likely to clash.

These constant punishments had their effect on Billy. It became clear to him that when surrounded by girls, if a fight erupted, no matter what the cause, he would be seriously punished and humiliated. He became afraid to fight for any reason. For the rest of his life, he had a complex that if he fought, everyone would be against him and he would be terribly humiliated.

Billy was often sent on errands at Polly Cary's convenience; this he resented, but Natalie thought everyone should be generous. It appeared to Billy that no one considered that Polly Cary, the older sister, should ever have to do favors for him.

Polly Cary had gotten to know some of the students in the college. It was not long before they asked her to be the mascot for one of their classes. This involved many little ceremonies including one called Up the Hill. (The college buildings were on a height of land with a beautiful view.) From as early as age three, Billy did not understand why he was excluded from all the activities Polly was invited to join. To make matters worse, Polly Cary teased him incessantly when, on rare occasions, such as putting on a child's play, Billy was included.

Someone had once given Billy a handsome book, *Wild Animals of North America*, beautifully illustrated by Louis Agassiz Fuertes. This appealed to him immensely. He read every account of each animal. As a result, he was eager to explore the woods, fields, and streams nearby.

He also greatly enjoyed walks with the family at Christmas. They would cover many miles of landscape looking for a Christmas tree and gathering holiday decorations. Mistletoe hung high in the tree tops, therefore out of their reach, but there were other pretty items of use lower down. There were red berries, which were also hard to reach, on a western facing hillside, so thickly overgrown with all manner of bushes, briars, and rocks. However, Billy made his way by following an old railroad right-of-way, then made it down the bank and across the swamp at the bottom, returning triumphantly with the branches of berries.

One Christmas the family went out to gather trailing cedar for decoration. They went quite a distance, beyond the large lake and into the virgin forest near the foot of Paul's Mountain. The trees were misty, some with mistletoe. The trailing cedar was lovely: long tendrils of bright green miniature plumes stretching through the dull brown carpet of damp dead leaves which covered the ground. In the distance, an owl was hooting. The big, beautiful, mysterious woods—Billy never forgot his love of them.

It was around this time that Billy began to sketch familiar objects such as the family cat, the silver teapot, and the house. However, designs were his favorite: houses, automobiles, and, later, airplanes, submarines, gasoline engines, guns, and railroad lines. He also happily constructed mini canal systems to drain the mud puddles in the back road. When his father brought the news that the Lusitania had been sunk, Billy made a diagram of that. He was becoming proficient at these sketches. They were all solo games, however, nothing suitable for playing with anyone else.

A history professor at the college whose family also had been connected with some of the former large land holding families of the old state had become a great friend of the Dew family. Billy overheard her say that his father's family had been virtually ruined by the Civil War (Confederate bonds), and that William himself, who was the youngest brother, had been particularly hard hit. When the slaves were set free, they immediately left. However, it was not long before most of them returned, unable to survive on their own. So William's parents had to feed them at a time when they had little for themselves. The plantation was unable to survive. The children were undernourished. The youngest, being William, was born at a terrible time. He grew up in an atmosphere of gloom, both at home and at their friends' homes. Many of the Southern gentry were very highly educated. Some were more likely able to recite the Odes of Horace than to succeed in the then-contemporary world.

William had entered the University in pre-law, but before he reached law school the money ran out. His future seemed bleak. To add to this, undernourishment had taken its toll. He was not very strong.

During these unhappy times, many turned to religion and to a very strict Victorian moral code. They also looked back fondly on happier pre-war days. The constant realization that they could no longer afford to do many things often produced a very negative mindset. William even took a dim view of medical innovations. Surgery was an invention of the devil, or, at least of the Yankees.

Their doctor had sometime before found that Billy had a bad tonsil condition. Natalie pleaded with William to allow an operation, but he wouldn't hear of it.

A number of years later, a crisis was brewing. William and Natalie thought the children were outgrowing Natalie's little school. Polly Cary was now eleven years old, and they thought they could afford to send her off to an Episcopal school. Billy, however, was the problem. He was too young to go off to school. Amherst was one of the poorest public schools in the state, and it didn't even have indoor plumbing. It was also four miles away. However, the county had finally gotten a bus to replace the ancient horse-drawn school wagon.

Natalie was disturbed about all this, and in secret, conferred with her brother Clayton Manson. "Billy is delicate, and has grown up almost entirely without the company of other boys to socialize. I do not know how he'll get along with these rough country types. Also, we do not want him learning to use foul language as they do. He has spent little time with his father, only at meals and sometimes in the evening before William goes to bed. William works like a slave to keep us going. They say he has done a very fine job here at the college. The place looks beautiful and appears to be making the grade financially, which has taken a lot of time. He has never really taken great interest in Billy. He is interested in the church, and follows financial affairs very closely. But he is tired when he comes home at night, and pays little attention to the children."

Clayton said he had noticed the child had always

seemed backward and very bashful. He said Billy was also small for his age and did not appear very strong.

Natalie hesitated, then reluctantly said, "As you know, he needs a tonsil operation. William has a terrible aversion to surgery, and I cannot get him to allow it. Dr. Sandidge says he has never seen a worse need for it. William is very kindly. From time to time he even helps people around the place, but he has never been able to accept the new concept of surgery."

"We have plenty of room in our house. Do you think William would let us take Billy for the winter and send him to the Lynchburg schools?"

"I have already asked William that. He said no. He wants to raise his own son."

That evening Natalie, very disturbed, discussed the situation with her husband. "I am afraid Billy will be quite unhappy at Amherst school. He has only been exposed to girls until now, and he is not very strong. Amherst is a backward country school, and most of the children who go there are equally backward. Many of them are nice children, but they do not have the values that we have tried to instill in Billy. Polly Cary will probably do very well at Chatham. The other girls there have been brought up in a similar way and come from refined families. Billy will be at a terrible disadvantage at Amherst. All the boys in the school have been there for years and are completely accustomed to it. Besides, they are rough, tough farm boys. The way we have brought up Billy, he would be far from falling in with them. If there were just some way we could break him in gradually. Maybe we could still come up with an alternative—somewhere we could send him where he would be with...well, more refined children that he might befriend."

William replied, "He has been with girls too much already. He has to learn to get along with the boys. If he doesn't, it will only get worse as time goes on."

Billy's fate was set.

CHAPTER 2

September the eighth, when school started, dawned clear and pleasant. Billy awoke early and lay in bed listening to the faraway sounds of the local freight putting on a car. He dressed and went into his parents' room with some questions.

His father said, "You will see all sorts of children at this school. Just remember you do not have to do all the things they do and/or say. If any of them use bad language, you don't have to use it too."

Natalie wanted to go to the school and make a few arrangements for Billy. Mrs. Martindale, the farm manager's kindly wife, had errands to run in Amherst, and agreed to take Natalie and Billy with her in her buggy. (The Dews did not yet have a car.) Billy rode in the back with his legs hanging over the ledge, watching the red clay dirt road go by under his feet.

They arrived some time before the children lined up and filed into the building. Billy stood awkwardly alone, then he merged into a large group, hoping not to be conspicuous. There was an angry argument going on with much cursing and use of words he had never heard before. It appeared a fight was about to start between two boys somewhat larger than himself. He was so upset that he needed to go to the bathroom. The only plumbing facility at the school was one drinking fountain in the hallway. The latrines were outdoors, without plumbing: the boys on one side of the school, the girls on the other, each fairly far from the main building. He went to the latrine, but it was indescribably filthy and the flies were abominable. The odor was such that he realized why it was some distance from the main building. There were a number of boys inside it; their loud conversation was repulsive to him. Billy could not make himself go in.

That evening Billy did not want any dinner. He stayed in his room. He told his mother he would not go back to school the next day. She sent him some dinner by Polly Cary, and he tried to eat it.

Natalie made a tearful plea to William on her son's behalf, but to no avail. In the morning, Billy still refused to go to the school, so William took charge. He descended on Billy in no uncertain fashion and simply laid him out verbally. Billy was afraid of his father, and now was more upset than he had been the day before. William accused his son of being a sissy and wanting to remain attached to his mother's apron strings.

Billy felt alone and without recourse. He went to school.

Before school and during the recesses, he huddled in the largest groups of children, attempting to be alone in the crowd. There were no organized athletics, and Billy did not have the vaguest idea how to play any of the simple games the children sometimes played.

In a game called "black horse" some boys, known as black horses, were stationed in a certain area. Others would try to run through it, and if the black horses could succeed in tackling them, or in some fashion stopping them, then they too became black horses. The game continued until virtually everyone became a black horse. This was a rough game played by strong, tough country boys. It was not like anything Billy had seen before. He was bashful and could not get up his nerve to try it.

After the balling out his father had given him the first day, Billy was afraid to say he was unhappy at the school. He simply submitted like a miserable, dumb animal, remaining silent at home and nearly so at school.

The other children on the school bus were those of the plumber, the carpenter, the stable hand, etc. They lived a mile or so away from the Dews. No one had ever told Billy that they were of lower social strata, but he could not help sensing this division as he grew up. On the school bus, this condition was reversed. Billy was the outcast, and the others the bedraggled leaders. Billy did not know how to cope with them at all. He found himself a seat beside the driver, Mr. Wray, and took it every day.

His mother could tell that Billy was inordinately unhappy in the school and it appeared that there was not much she could do about it.

Billy's father delved deeply into the best in literature, particularly biography and historical subjects. His family, in more prosperous days, had been important in politics and education in the Old South. William could never quite get the South's defeat out of his mind, and studied every angle of the Civil War.

He had to realize that one could no longer expect the things that had been normal in days gone by. He was concerned about Billy at Amherst, but he had long ago had to realize that the "essentials of life" were all one could expect, and that Billy's difficulties were only more of the "slings and arrows" of the times in the South.

In secret, it galled William that his good job at the college was mainly due to Clayton Manson.

Clayton had been a success from the start. He was good looking and athletic. He had been the light heavy-weight boxing champion of the university and had belonged to one of the strongest fraternities, Beta. He had returned to Lynchburg to practice law and had soon formed his own firm, which by now was the strongest in the town. Clayton had served as executor of the estate of the family who had bequeathed their entire fortune to create Sweet Briar College after the death of their only child, a daughter. He had put it together, started the project, and was still Chairman of the Board. He was happily married to the daughter of the chairman of the town's principle tobacco company, a powerful outfit. The marriage was, however, childless. Clayton had always wanted a son. He would very much have liked Billy to live at his home during the winters and go to the Lynchburg schools. William was too proud to let him do so.

Polly Cary had by now gone off to the prep school, Chatham Episcopal Institute, later called Chatham Hall, some hundred miles away. She was the youngest child there, but she was accustomed to being the leader, and being very bright and pretty, soon made a place for herself with the other very young girls. Her letters home gave the impression she was extremely happy at the school.

At this time, there was a tragedy at the college. Dr. Pruden, the principal, was badly hurt in a car wreck and had to resign. William recommended a recent bright Sweet Briar graduate, Nan Powell, to succeed him. The recommendation was accepted, and she became the principal.

It happened one day that Natalie and her sister, Mrs. Mattie Massie, were inspired to drive the hundred-odd miles to Chatham for a visit with Polly Cary. In those days, there were few through highways and no road maps. Billy went along and was fascinated by what they called "navigation," which consisted of trying to follow a list of instructions such as: At Ford Otter Creek, turn left at the first red barn, go one mile, turn right at the crossroads at the top of the hill. They resulted in several uncertain interpretations, backtracking, and unhappiness as to whether they were driving in the right or wrong direction; however, the three finally arrived safely.

Polly Cary was happily playing basketball. She enthusiastically showed her visitors the campus and buildings. As usual, she soon managed to play a trick on Billy. She showed her mother and aunt her dormitory and room, places from which Billy was excluded. He was waiting at the foot of the stairs when he was engulfed by a small group of girls, and was, as planned, most embarrassed.

He had better luck at lunch in the dining room when one of the younger girls winked at him. Billy noticed she was very pretty, and he was duly fascinated.

Clayton, both because of his duties as Chairman of the Board at Sweet Briar College, and because he was greatly interested in it, visited as often as he could. The usual way of making the 15-mile trip from Lynchburg to Sweet Briar was by train. The more affluent people were beginning to own automobiles. It was not long before Clayton appeared in a new, soft green Cadillac. It was beautiful, with enormous shining brass headlights, a mahogany dashboard, a top which could be let down in fine weather, and which was reinforced by great leather straps from the front corners down to the front fenders. It also had a chauffeur with whom Billy soon made friends.

Clayton would, from time to time, have dinner in the

Apartment House, where most of the single female faculty members lived. Many of them were highly educated, but were not really great advertisements for women in education, something fairly new in those days. Clayton was good company; the ladies enjoyed his visits considerably.

At the Dew's home, Natalie was also good company, very hospitable, and of a sympathetic disposition. Lonely people on the campus frequently dropped by. Among these visitors was Dr. Harley, a maiden lady. One day she stopped by during lunch. She was discussing her favorite subject: archaeological digs in Africa, and her plan, whenever she retired, to join one of these digs. She then strayed to her own youth, and how, as a child, she was playing in the street and was run over by a large bread wagon and left as a cripple for life. Her voice almost broke as she mentioned old age coming on and ending whatever life she had managed to have. It was she who had given Billy the book *Wild Animals of North America*, and other handsome gifts.

Another tragic, heroic figure to Billy was Meta Glass, the next president of the college. She had been a brilliant student, was the half-sister of an outstanding senator, Carter Glass, and had grown up in Lynchburg. Her resumé was impressive. Professionally, she had scaled all the heights to which anyone could aspire. The extraordinary old house, which was now the president's house, in the beautiful big garden, would never be more suitably tenanted.

In her way, Meta was quite handsome, but not of a type which men would find appealing, and she had never been married. Her face seemed to speak of brilliance, determination, courage, and tragedy.

She was an excellent speaker on formal occasions and a credit to the college. But there was a problem. One evening when the college was reopening after the summer, and all the girls were gathered in the auditorium, she was making an informal speech, welcoming them to the new college year, wishing them luck, and hoping they would all be happy. At this point, her voice began to leave her, and she, on the verge of tears, completely broke down and had to be seated. There was no doubt that some great unhappiness in her past had never really healed, that her life of scholarship and endeavor had not really taken the place of home and fireside.

The girls had a proverb that careers were fine, but you could not run your fingers through their hair.

CHAPTER 3

It was the Dew family's custom to spend the month of June in Wytheville, Virginia. Natalie and the children went up first, and William joined them for the last week. William's father's health had been ruined in the Confederate Army during the war, and, after the failure of the plantation, he had moved to Wytheville. There he had started a school, which had done fairly well. He had two sons and a daughter. One was William at Sweet Briar, another Harry, a very successful doctor in Lynchburg, and the daughter was named Bland.

During World War I, Harry had died of the flu. His wife was already dead, leaving five children: Henry, Tom, Braxton, Virginia, and Lelia. Miss Bland had taken the children and devoted her life to raising them. After the senior Mr. Dew's death, the school had folded, but there had been one ace still in the deck. In the very hot summers, it was nice and cool up in the mountains at Wytheville. Many lovely people from the far south came there to dodge the heat and spend the summer. Miss Bland's house became a mecca for them. All of the business was handled in the most gentlemanly of ways, and enough money was provided to support the family. Henry attended Washington and Lee and Massachusetts Institute of Technology; Tom went to Virginia Military Institute; and Braxton attended Washington and Lee.

In June, before the super paying guests started arriving, Miss Bland was sometimes visited by old friends from southeastern Virginia. It happened one year that a relative, Elsie Bowlie, was there. Her sister, Jessie Ball, had recently married Alfred Irenee (A.I.) duPont, a glamorous marriage from the bankrupt Southern viewpoint.

Elsie and General Bowlie had a son, Thomas, close in age to Billy. It happened that, after visiting Aunt Bland, she was going on to Nemours to visit her sister Jessie. Thomas was already there, and she had the inspiration to take Billy along for a week at Nemours.

Other than Sweet Briar, Billy had seen hardly anything but the rudimentary buildings where he had lived: Amherst, Wytheville, and Lynchburg, where his uncle Clayton had a moderate, but very fine Victorian house, his aunt Sally's house next door, Maurice Moore's house (Clayton's brother-in-law), and Garney's house in Rivermont.

Nemours was a different matter. There was a wall about eight feet high all around it. The wall was covered with colored glass chips, and was several miles long. Through the main gate, one started up a fine gravel road. It followed a long, landscaped area, with a pool about 50 yards long at the bottom, and a classic balustrade around curved ends. From the pool to the house, there was a distance of more than 100 yards, with a few steps in it, and hedges on both sides, perhaps 40 yards wide. Beyond the pool and from the house, there was the most elaborate patterned garden, with sculpture, extending to the outside wall, a distance of perhaps another 100 yards.

The house, with 52 rooms in all, had been built by a

fine New York architect early in the century. On the side toward the large pool was a two-story porch with high classic columns and a finely fitted stone floor. A majestic iron door, with glass between the well-worked out metal, led into a vestibule, with another door toward the house. Inside was an enormous entrance hall with alternating black and white marble tiles. On each side were powder rooms. Toward the left were arches leading into a stair hall, in which the gradual, wide stairs went completely around and opened to a hall above. Another entrance led into a hall, which, in turn, gave access to the living and dining rooms. On the right were the library, the small parlor, a large play room with windows looking on a formal garden outside. In the basement, Billy mainly remembered there being a bowling alley.

The dining room table was glorious: large, with silver pheasants; enormous, beautiful silver candlesticks; all sorts of small containers filled with mints and candy and various glasses at each place.

Billy was so dumbfounded, he hardly knew what to do. Cousin Jessy went all out to make him feel at home, just as she would have in the old days at Epping Forest.

After dinner, the group retired to the living room. Jessy's adopted daughter, Denise, then only three or four years old, was there, gleefully climbing to the top of the large pieces of heavy, beautifully finished furniture, and sliding down.

Thomas Wright was there, not saying much.

Mr. duPont was also there. He had previously had an accident while sport shooting with one of his employees; the hired man had accidentally shot him. Partially because of this, Mr. duPont was now quite deaf. He had a large speaking tube, which one spoke into. When introduced to

Billy, the child was handed his end of the tube. Billy was so frightened that he couldn't think of anything to say.

In spite of these overwhelming surroundings, Billy and Thomas amused themselves very well. They drove a pony cart with two very gentle ponies. Every morning before breakfast they would go for a dip in the large pool. And then there was the garage, which housed 14 automobiles. They inspected it carefully.

Jessie Ball had fit into her new role with perfection. She did whatever she could possibly do to heal the rift with the other duPonts; she ran the house to perfection, and she encouraged, shielded, and helped her husband.

At the start of the Great Depression, Mr. duPont bought up much of the real estate and half the small banks in the state of Florida, which was then almost a rustic outpost. He started the Almours Security Company. The word Almours was taken from his name and the estate: Alfred duPont de Nemours.

In Florida, Jessie added her brother, Edward Ball, to her social group. Eddie Ball lived a long life, and became a financial challenge to Florida. When he died, Almours was worth around two million dollars.

The group also frequently invited Henry Dew down from New York for weekends at Nemours. Mr. duPont liked him and strongly suggested he leave the Union Carbide Company he was with and join them in Florida. Henry finally accepted and became a vice president.

Billy had now caught a glimpse of the Big World, which later so fascinated him. But for then it was too much. Mrs. duPont drove him to the station when he left. On the train he began to feel ill. This worsened, and he came down with intestinal flu. He was sick with this for several days. During this time, he became depressed. His father had once called him a sissy, and he was unable to let go of the hurt from that incident. One night, he attended a meeting at Mr. Peyton Evans' house in Amherst, which was supposed to be for the young boys of the church. They had discussed a camping trip on the river for all of them. He remembered this, and cringed with fear. He couldn't get the word "sissy" out of his mind. It was days before he recovered.

It further happened not long afterward that William and Natalie went to New York for a vacation. William loved grand opera.

His office received a frantic phone call from the school. Polly Cary had acute appendicitis. The closest adequate hospital and operating room was in Lynchburg. To try driving over the roads would have been hopelessly slow. It was necessary to put her on the first train and hope for the best.

The gears began to turn in Lynchburg with Clayton in charge. The doctors could not legally operate without William and Natalie's permission. They were not at their hotel in New York. There seemed no way to contact them. There was also fear that were the doctors able to contact William, he would oppose the surgery. William's well known feeling against surgery was frightening.

Clayton was forced to work feverishly to concoct documents to permit the operation without parental permission. The hospital would have an ambulance at the station.

Meanwhile, Polly Cary, in great pain, was on an improvised bed in the baggage car of the local train, which was under orders to make the trip in the shortest possible time.

By the time the train clanged into the station, the appendix had burst, but Clayton had arranged enough pressure on the hospital and doctors that they accepted the operation on his responsibility.

Polly Cary survived.

This unfortunate incident was in the early spring. William, during the few days when Polly Cary's life swayed in the balance, went through the fires of hell realizing what would have happened if he had forbidden the operation. He did not believe he would have done so, but the incident softened his prejudice against surgery, and he decided to permit Billy's much needed tonsillectomy. Both children stayed out of school for the rest of the term. Billy's health began slowly to improve.

The following year a new farm manager was hired at Sweet Briar. He had a son, George, somewhat older than Billy, and also a nephew, Billy Middleton, who lived with the family. Billy was able to make friends with them and things began to improve for him.

They soon began to explore the 8,000 acres of the college land. One Saturday, they walked to Bear Mountain, higher and considerably farther away than Paul's Mountain. There was a large brook that began where the water tumbled down from the spillway, at the large stone dam. It held the water in the lake, and was used for drinking water at the college. This ran through deep woods and connected with another strong stream, which drained the wild area between Paul's and Bear Mountains. This formed yet a considerable stream, which the boys thought could be fished. Alongside these streams, the boys found many animal tracks: fox, raccoon, muskrat, weasel, mink, and others still more fascinating, which they couldn't identify. One of the boys had gotten a price list from a country store quoting what could be gotten for trapped furs: Tanned muskrat skins, $5.00; Skunks, $10.00; Raccoon, $15.00; Fox, $25.00, Mink, $35.00; and the clincher, Silver fox, $400.00. They decided to run a trap line.

The boys were fascinated with exploring the woods and streams, searching for fox dens and mink tracks. There was a rumor that someone had seen a silver fox somewhere in the vicinity. There were some small marshes at places around the lake, and they seemed full of muskrats.

By pooling their resources, the boys raised several dollars and purchased some traps. Over the next few weeks, results were not sensational, but they managed to net several muskrats, an opossum, and a skunk. They had gotten an enormous amount of exercise and learned the locations of fox dens and streams in which mink traveled. In short, the boys had a glorious time.

The big, beautiful hills, virgin woods, and streams seemed to spell adventure and endless interest. One day, the boys brought a gun along. An enormous owl was flushed from a tree and George shot at it. It continued to fly away, unharmed. However, in a thicket some forty or so yards away, immediately after the shot, they heard the loud snapping of a stick, as if some heavier animal had been frightened by the shot and broken it in fleeing. They cautiously reconnoitered, but could find nothing.

Could it have been a deer, a bear, or—even—a mountain lion? The nearest place where deer resided was a whole county and river away. There were a few bear on the high mountains, which could be clearly seen to the north. Mountain lions were said to silently shadow people in the woods, but no one knew for sure whether or not they were extinct in the state. The boys' imaginations were sparked, and they were quite excited.

CHAPTER 4

The season merged from summer into winter. There had not yet been more than a dusting of snow, but late one afternoon William declared the wind was from the east, and there was a biting chill in the air. After dinner, the flakes began to fall. Billy was excited and went out on the porch several times to see how much snow was falling. By morning, it was too deep to go to school.

Billy wanted to visit the trap lines, but the snow was too deep.

The next day was no better. William told Billy he should go as soon as possible and spring all the traps, otherwise something might be trapped alive for several days. On the third, day Billy managed to reach the traps and be back by dark.

Two or three days later, Billy saw the other boys at school and told them that he had sprung the traps, and suggested that, before the snow melted, they go out and look for tracks in the snow and re-set the traps.

"It's too late," said George. "We went out yesterday. Someone found your tracks, followed them, found the traps and stole them. Unless we can get more traps, we are ruined for this winter."

Gloom descended on the boys. It was hoped William

would donate more traps, but this didn't happen.

As Christmas approached, the boys at school became interested in fireworks. This belatedly provided something in common for Billy with the other boys. At Wood's General Store, there were inch-and-a-half squibs, two-inch boomers, and three-inch salutes. Billy began to stop by when he felt rich and make small purchases. It was beautiful to go out in front of the house and explode a few before breakfast.

The big deal, however, was to be Christmas morning. There was much talk regarding pyrotechnical exploits to be performed then. Billy laid in a good supply: many of the squibs, a good number of boomers, and a small, but impressive number of the more expensive and powerful salutes.

The morning of the planned events arrived. Before sunrise, Billy was out with his ammunition. The morning was clear; the hills and valleys seemed bathed in the soft light. The plan was to greet the first rays of the sun with a volley of salutes.

The sun was almost up when Billy viewed his mother, obviously hurriedly dressed, coming out of the house with the manner of a self-sacrificing angel.

"We can't have any firecrackers this morning. Polly Cary was at a party last night and needs her sleep." Billy angrily flung his ammunition on the ground and walked away. Many faint booms were heard from distant houses, where small boys were able to be small boys.

Billy was still sulking while opening his gifts. Polly Cary was radiantly happy and bubbling with conversation.

The next fall, Billy was to go to the Virginia Episcopal School, a new Episcopal prep school, less than 20 miles away, just outside of Lynchburg. The principal, William Pendleton, a fine minister, was from a family that dated back to early colony days, and whose family William's had known for generations. The previous principal, who had been there the four years since the school had opened, was now a bishop. William and Natalie were very happy that Billy was going to VES. Everything would be all right from now on, they believed.

The school consisted of three main buildings. There was the main one, in which were classrooms, several dormitory floors, the dining room (in the basement), and the school offices. Another smaller dormitory building called the West Dorm contained two classrooms in the basement. A third building, the gymnasium, also had a few bedrooms.

The school's internal mechanical engineering plan was disastrous. The furnace was in the cellar of the main building, which was well heated. Underground pipes carried the heated steam to the other two buildings, which were abominably heated, if at all.

Some of the youngest new boys, including Billy, were put in the west building, on the first floor. The September weather was warm and pleasant, so no heat was needed; this seemed a good spot.

During Billy's first night, he dreamed of familiar things back home, and then of the school. He had the bleak feeling that the old pleasures would be no more, that there would be nothing but the strange, forbidding life at this school, which would last three quarters of a year. He was awakened from this by the forboding sound of the school bell.

In spite of the dream, the shock of this new life was mild compared to that at Amherst, but there were still serious problems. The long tables in the refectory became like the former school bus: Billy still had nothing in common with the other boys. He had actually greatly enjoyed the brief company of his two or three former friends with whom he had the trap line, but at VES he was lost in the shuffle. His attempts to even talk to the other boys were a failure. He neither knew anything about, nor yet had any interest in, the various school activities.

VES had a large study hall in the main building. Every boy had a desk there; it was a home base. They were expected to be there at all times during the mornings and early afternoons unless they were in class. They were all supposed to be there again from 8 o'clock until 10 o'clock in the evenings. However, anyone who averaged 90 or better (out of 100) for one month would be excused from evening study hall for the next month, and instead assigned with some other boy to a classroom to study. This was preferred to sitting quietly in the study hall. After his first month, Billy qualified for this privilege.

This success was most fortunate. Billy was assigned with the youngest boy in school, Reverdy Winfree, who was a few months younger than he and a nice, intelligent boy. They got along well, and Reverdy soon invited Billy to play basketball with a small group who went down to the gymnasium between dinner and study hall. Billy, who had never played before, had his troubles, but he made an amazing discovery: these games were a lot of fun. Suddenly, he started enjoying school.

VES required the boys to exercise. If they weren't on some team, they had to work out in the gym, or walk or run outside. Basketball season soon started, so there wasn't any room in the gym except after dinner. The varsity team had preference. The few minutes of after-dinner basketball were not enough to qualify as exercise. Billy had to settle for walking as his official exercise program.

The new school's budget did not yet have much room for medical matters. This department consisted of two rooms in an old frame farm house, which had been retained as a professor's residence. The pleasant history professor, Mr. Ladd, lived upstairs. The first-floor health facility was manned by a dim-witted practical nurse. A sick student's fate depended solely on her, unless she decided to call a doctor from Lynchburg.

As autumn advanced toward winter, the West Dorm grew colder and colder. Taking a shower was a rugged experience. As happens in most schools, before long someone had a cold and the contagion spread through the whole school. Billy, still a little weak, became ill.

The ordinary miseries of a bad cold lingered a week or so, then unfortunate complications ensued. Mumps-like symptoms developed, and Billy went to the infirmary. The doctor from Lynchburg disagreed with the tentative mumps diagnosis, yet Billy's moderate fever continued. He was returned to the West Dorm and classes. He felt worse and went back to see the nurse. He had no luck there this time.

"Don't be a baby, Dew, go on back and stop bothering me," said the nurse.

Billy then had to resume hiking for the required exercise program. The day was damp and rainy. There was a little ice on the tree branches. He walked four miles.

The next day he had a terrible cough. Luckily, it was Friday, and he was going home for the weekend.

By the following day, he had a fever of 106 degrees.

Natalie, greatly alarmed, went immediately to the college infirmary to get Dr. Harley. The nurse said the doctor was sick in bed. She explained that because it was snowing outside, Dr. Harley would be risking his own health if he ventured out. However, the nurse agreed to give the doctor Natalie's message.

Natalie returned home almost in despair. Unless a

physician could be brought in from Lynchburg—at least a matter of several hours—Billy would go without qualified medical treatment.

Billy could see out of the window from his bed. In a few brief minutes, there came Dr. Harley, limping through the snow.

Billy had double pneumonia. In those days, there were no "wonder drugs." There was no way of knowing whether or not he would survive.

At the Dew's home, every room had a fireplace. A fire was built in Billy's room so that the draft would constantly pull in air from the rest of the house. A chamois vest was made for him to ensure constant warmth. By the next day, William had been able to get around-the-clock nurses to look after his son.

The climax came at the end of the fifth day. Around 2 a.m., the night nurse heard William walking around; she tiptoed out of the bedroom and told him, "The news is good; I think he is going to make it."

Although Billy regained his health, for many months he was left with serious heart problems. He did not return to VES that spring, and he was forbidden to take strenuous exercise. By late spring, Billy started studying by himself, and during the summer, made trips to the school for tutoring. Before school started again, VES gave him special exams, which he was able to pass.

The next fall Billy returned to school. He was still forbidden to participate in strenuous physical activity, and having been more or less alone for several months had not been good for him. Other than to study and join an athletic team, there was little to do at school. Billy was excused from the exercise program. He grew unhappy, as he now had less in common with the other boys. Also, his contemporaries, now a little older, had grown a little more sophisticated, and he had not. He was not able to concentrate, and although he had passed his make-up exams, the time he had missed did not help.

Billy felt he was an outcast at the school and worried about it constantly. He couldn't help realizing the contrast between this and Polly Cary's scintillating record at Chatham Hall. He never again qualified to be excused from study hall.

Billy's second year finally drew to a close. His heart fibrillation had entirely vanished, and restrictions on exercise had been lifted. In the horrific year he had just experienced, he had had plenty, indeed, too much time to think. He remembered the few basketball games and the "black horse" games at Amherst that he never had the nerve to try. He was determined to go out for athletics the next year.

Billy was not nearly large and strong enough to try for the varsity football team; some of those players weighed in at close to 200 pounds. There were smaller teams that competed locally. The Mites at 100 pounds or less, the Midgets at 120 or less, and the Juniors at 140 or less. Billy fit into the Midgets.

The football players were, of course, the heroes of the school, and the weekly varsity games against some of the other prep schools in the state were the highlight of the fall season. Billy's little team in the City League was a miniature copy. Yet the daily practices for it could be very exciting. Gone was the extreme depression of the year before.

Billy tried desperately to qualify for the little team. When the first real game started, he was so nervous that he was virtually in a daze. He succeeded in making a tackle, and from then on it went much better. By the end of the season, he was playing reasonably well.

In the spring, came track season. Billy, not fast enough for the sprints and having no expertise at the field events, tried the half-mile. VES had a good track coach. In the first meet, a Triangular Meet between VES and two smaller prep schools, VES trounced the others soundly. In the half-mile, it took first, second, and third places. At some distance behind the first three, but still ahead of the competition, came Billy.

At VES, as in many prep schools, particularly small ones, the teams were "It." Because of this small success, Billy found he was becoming a part of the place. Instead of hearing the cheering section yell, disapprovingly, "Come on, Dew," it began to be a more friendly, "Come on, Billy!" He was no longer an outcast. A successful second year at VES concluded, and Billy went home for the summer.

During the summer, there was not much for the young people to do at Sweet Briar. Long afternoons at the lake, fishing once or twice a week, and little else. There was plenty of time to read and the privilege of using the college library.

When Billy was 14, his father bought the family's first car. William, no longer so young, did not exactly take to it like a duck to water. The second day it was there, the very nice farm manager, who was instructing William in its operation, drove it to a large grassy field and let Billy try it. He was so small he had to have a stout pillow behind him to reach the pedals. He first drove it 15 feet and stopped for a breather. He was absolutely thrilled with it. He started again, managed to shift gears, drove it the length of the field, emerged on the road, and drove it all around the farm with utmost pleasure. From then on, he, in spite of his 14 years, was the star driver of the family.

Polly Cary, very bright, was now almost 16, and had just graduated from Chatham. Among the many honors she earned was the medal for "Best All-Around Girl" in the school. Her mother was suitably worried about the total lack of social life at Sweet Briar during the summer. At Amherst, four miles away, there were frequent small parties, usually "Victrola dances" for the small and minimally sophisticated group of teenagers there. Billy's success with the new car gave her ideas. Billy should be taught to dance. Polly Cary, no Ginger Rogers herself, commenced the job.

The idea was that Billy, age 14, could take his sister to enough parties to get her started. Polly Cary was quite good looking, but was totally unaccustomed to boys. Because of her strict upbringing and serious nature, and already well-educated mind, the local swains didn't know exactly how to cope with her. Some of them, regrettably, were afraid of her. They simply didn't know what approach to take. They considered her cold as ice.

Four miles to Amherst, four miles back, twice an evening, was a lot of driving for local boys if they could get access to an automobile. So Billy, evening after evening, ferried Polly Cary to Amherst and remained there with her. At first, this made him feel very grown up. It was something new and exciting. He tried to dance, without much luck. It became more and more obvious that the girls were making excuses, when he invited them to dance. The evenings grew longer and longer, and it became obvious to Billy that he was only a chauffeur for Polly Cary. He grew completely sick of it.

During the summers, Mr. Worthington, the professor of languages at Sweet Briar, was away operating a certain business enterprise. It happened that his brother and family from Washington, D.C., took possession of his house for six weeks. They had a son about Billy's age, and the two boys became inseparable friends. Life consisted of going for the paper every morning to see if the Senators had won the ball game, practicing baseball, and playing a miniature baseball game they had invented themselves.

When the Worthingtons returned to Washington, Billy was invited to go back with them for a week. This was pure heaven. No one was bossing him around. Whatever they did was the main event of the day. If they were going to the zoo, that was it. If there was a ball game, that was it. They watched one ball game with Walter Johnson pitching for the Senators and Ty Cobb at center field for Detroit. Walter Johnson pitched a no-hitter through the first out in the ninth inning. It was thrilling.

They went once to a museum and the Capital building. To make it perfect, there was complete relief from running errands for and playing a very poor "second fiddle" to Polly Cary.

Upon Billy's return, on the way back from the station, his mother brought up the subject of a party they were going to have for Polly Cary. Polly informed Billy he was going to make several trips to Amherst bringing guests and taking them back. Billy, emboldened by the pleasure he had had in Washington, was livid at the humiliation of being once more ordered around by Polly Cary. He objected furiously. At least in the past, his mother had told him with reasonable diplomacy when he had to do something for Polly Cary. He could not stand the idea of being given orders by Polly Cary herself and of chauffeuring these friends of hers, to whom he meant nothing. He further objected to going to a party where he would be reminded he was one person too many.

Billy's objections got him nowhere. He was told he would have to do it, which put him in a foul humor. Being back where everything was run by and for his sister was just too much. He refused to talk about his trip. The more he made objections to the chauffeuring, the more he couldn't stand the idea. No one considered having Polly Cary do a favor for Billy, both to diffuse the situation and, just possibly, to show him some respect. There was simply no precedent for any such consideration.

When Billy was driven back to VES he still would not enter into the conversation. When they got there, he simply walked away without saying good-bye.

For weeks he didn't write home. In the past, he had gone home for frequent weekends. No more.

Natalie wrote him pleading letters. Even Polly Cary, now a freshman at Sweet Briar, wrote a nice letter trying to straighten things out.

Finally, Henry, William's very prosperous nephew from Florida, came by Sweet Briar for two days. He and William drove over to VES to see Billy. This was a complete surprise. In Billy's previous years at the school, his father had frequently come close by to play golf, but had never stopped by to see Billy. Henry didn't know about the problems, and William hadn't paid much attention to them. This unexpected visit broke the ice.

The next year, Polly Cary had a job as a counselor in Mr. Worthington's summer camp. The problem did not recur.

The next year at VES, his last, things improved for Billy. He actually had some friends. He led the school in trigonometry. He received a prize for excellence in French. He was an editor on the school paper. He played fairly well at football. At the end of one game, which they won, his teammates gave a cheer for him.

CHAPTER 5

Henry had sent from Florida a clipping about choosing a profession. One highly recommended was architecture. William and Natalie were impressed by it. Billy had shown strong creative talent, and had done very well in mathematics. VES had mainly emphasized the church and had no art department. Unfortunately, Billy's time there had been substantially wasted in the matter of his main talent, but this couldn't be helped. The subject of a career was discussed with him. He liked the idea and readily agreed. Actually, this meant for him "crossing the Rubicon"; he had never before had a choice in anything.

The obvious college choice for him was the University of Virginia. It was not far away, not atrociously expensive, had a great tradition of gentlemanly conduct, and one of the best honor systems in the world.

The university had a new and small department of architecture, which had not yet become a separate school, but had previously had a very distinguished head, Fiske Kimball, and was now getting another one, Edmund Cambell. Perhaps the university's greatest asset was the early nineteenth-century buildings, designed by Thomas Jefferson, which were internationally famous. They made a strong impression on Billy. There seemed no doubt that this was the place for him.

In his last years at VES, one of the friends Billy made was William Cabell, who also came from an old family in the state. He too had gone through VES with little spending money. His mother had been widowed early in life, and been left with little money, and three sons to raise and educate. She had left her former job for one in the office of the university, and had taken a house there to greatly reduce the cost of her sons' college education. To further help with costs, she took in several other carefully selected boys, of which Billy was one.

The university's distinguished group of original buildings, reminiscent of Palladio's work, was frequently considered among the best in the world. The architectural school, although small and rather new, had built up some tradition, having been staffed by most able people. The present head was new, but had left a prestigious job to join the staff.

The university itself was in a stage of crisis. It was being overrun by boys from the northeastern states who could not get into the Ivy League colleges or who were not serious enough to try hard. This university, being partially supported by the state, was politically prevented from keeping its admission standards high enough to keep the poorer students out.

Most of the first-year courses in architecture particularly suited Billy. Among his favorite areas of learning were the principles of composition; locating points and planes in space; sketching and painting; advanced mathematics; and later in the year, making huge, shaded, highly finished drawings of designs for small architectural projects. By spring, Billy was tied for the top student in the class.

Billy made strides in other areas at UVA as well. There were two small fraternities in the architectural school. The better by far was the Scarab. Most of the best students in the school belonged to it. They were the leaders in every way. Some of them were brilliant. The best and most popular one, Laurence Anderson, finally won the Paris Prize, the most coveted national award of all.

Billy was invited to join Scarab and he was simply ecstatic.

He also continued his athletics. Early in the autumn, he went out for and made the cross-country team. One of the first races (3½ miles) of the season finished with a lap and a half in the stadium in front of the stands to entertain the spectators between halves of the Washington and Lee football game. Billy's part of it was more exciting than expected: as he re-entered the stadium, a friend paced him and told him that the score was tied, and if he beat the man in front of him he would win the meet for the university. The loud speakers took it up, and the home team crowd cheered for Billy. Both runners were in the agony of exhaustion. As they passed the stands for the second time, it sounded like the Kentucky Derby. Billy won by three feet.

He did not go out for cross-country again.

American architectural education, in the 1920's, was patterned after the French. The university permitted the Charette system for the large drawings, called Analytiques, which took around six weeks to do. A charette was actually, in French, a small cart. The boys at the Ecole des Beaux-Arts in Paris were no more systematic than the Americans; toward the end of the six weeks, they were seldom ready. When the final moment came to put their drawings on the charettes, which carried them to the Ecole to be judged, they, allegedly, sometimes ran along beside them in the street, still trying to finish the drawings.

"Charette Week" at the university consisted of staying up working most of the last few nights, trying hard to
finish. This was simply too much physically for Billy. In
the spring, around the end of a "Charette Week," in a practice mile race, Billy was unable to finish. The next morning he was in the hospital. His very bad cold/flu-like symptoms continued for several days, but his fever wouldn't go
away. The hospital was having difficulty diagnosing him.

After he had been in the hospital ten or so days in an
eight-man ward, Billy received a pleasant surprise. Suddenly, through the door trooped in a dozen or so young
men: the entire Scarab fraternity had come to visit him.

Back at Sweet Briar, Mr. Worthington was a good
friend of William's. He had a wide circle of friends, particularly in academia. One of his friends, Dr. Flippen, was
a professor of medicine at the university, and head of the
hospital. Mr. Worthington called and asked him to personally take Billy's case. The verdict: suspected TB.

Luckily, it was almost the end of the year. Billy had
not finished his last problem, but his grades were very
good. The head of the architectural school arranged to have
him do a small additional amount of work in several subjects, and passed him for the year.

Billy's fever subsided. He had to rest for three weeks
and be careful for a while. Once again, he was unable to
participate in athletics for half a year, but no more charettes
for the remainder of his college career.

Billy, when in school, particularly at VES, had at best,
never really felt at home. He had done extremely well in
his classes until his early pneumonia attack and was considerably above average even after it. He had never made
the grade with the other boys and had developed a deep
sense of inferiority. He had never felt that most of them

liked him. This was a constant nagging worry that made him unhappy. At VES there had been a constant emphasis on religion. But there was no one that a boy could talk to about something troubling like this.

At the university, things were considerably better for Billy. He enjoyed the school of architecture and it was nice living at the Cabell's home.

However, social fraternities were a problem. The customary procedure, approved and enforced by the interfraternity council, was that until a certain day early in the fall, no bids to fraternities could be given. On that day, a Sunday, for two hours in the afternoon, every member of the first-year class was to sit in his room and be available to receive bids. Billy, William Cabell, and the others in the house, were all there waiting. William received two bids; Billy received none.

William did not accept either of his bids. It would be expensive to join a fraternity, and, frankly, he thought he might do better later on. Neither bid was from a top fraternity.

Billy didn't realize what was really wrong. He looked and acted very young for his age. At one of the fraternities, which might have considered him, someone quipped, "How young *is* that guy?"

Billy tried to appear unconcerned, but in secret this was like turning a knife in an old wound. He sought refuge in his work and in the success he was having in the architectural school.

Since the old days at Amherst, Billy suffered from spells of depression. This was getting worse. However, there was another side to it. At times when he was very unhappy, some little thing would happen—someone he admired would speak to him in a friendly way, he would get a good grade, or perhaps he would remember something which cheered him up—and suddenly he would be in a wonderful, unreasonably happy mood. Billy realized he had bouts of depression followed by periods of euphoria.

He was depressed for days after the fraternity bidding day.

A young man from Lynchburg was a member of Billy's class whom he had known slightly for years and considered likable. He had joined a small fraternity. Later that year, he invited Billy and William to his fraternity house one evening.

The fraternity members turned on the charm. There were some good selling points for the fraternity. Two years before, its members had made one of the highest scholastic averages in the country. The star student in the architectural school, Ralph Gulley, who had recently graduated, had been a member. Also, members were the class poet, the star of the first-year boxing team, a socially prominent young man from New York, and two unusually nice young men from the deep South who were also top students.

Billy was impressed. Their interest in him was also balm for the wound of not receiving any bid at all on that terrible Sunday afternoon in October. In all his school experience, this was the first organization or group of people that had ever wanted him. Later, they gave Billy and William bids to join the fraternity.

William would have none of it. Billy wavered. He asked advice from an older student. He discussed it with the Cabells. He called his father, who said he would leave it with Billy; he knew that whatever he did would be right.

Mrs. Cabell advised him strongly not to join; two of the other young men in the house did the same.

Billy had been convinced by the picture of a glorious

fraternity that the members had painted. One evening, he went to the house and accepted the bid. Sterling Clairborne, from Georgia, welcomed him warmly. David Reese, from the North, simply looked glum.

It was not long before the "glorious" fraternity picture began to fade. The excellent scholars they had, including the architect Ralph Gulley, had graduated. The socially prominent New Yorker was indeed very rich, but was a no-good drunk. The class poet was a homosexual.

Billy made the best of it, but it became obvious that he had made a big mistake, which would hang around his neck for the next few years.

After Billy's required six-month rest, William Cabell asked him to go down to the gym and work out at the track with him. The old lure and glamour of athletics came back strongly. Few people in his new fraternity knew many people in other fraternities or around the college in general. The same applied to the architectural school. The gymnasium and the teams formed a bridge from all that. They meant excitement, glamour, new contacts. Billy decided to go out for track again.

In the architectural school, the students, five days a week, were supposed to be in the drafting room 2:30 - 5:30 p.m. This left no time for athletics. Another VES graduate, who had been named center on the mythical "All State Football Team," and was a star athlete in general, had to give it up entirely. Billy found he could leave the drawing a little early, go down to the nearby gymnasium and get a good workout before dinner. He frequently worked on weekends, so he could afford the time to do this. He really trained himself. It made him feel particularly good. He continued to increase difficulty in his workouts. He thought he might possibly make the track team.

The track coach, "Pop" Lannigan, had an excellent record at the university, but he was now old and things had gotten informal. Billy explained his problems to Pop, who agreed that he could try for the team while training himself in the afternoons, after the rest of the team had finished their practice.

Sometime during the winter, there was an indoor meet in another city, and the university was sending part of a team to it. William Cabell, a star hurdler, made the trip to run a special 300-yard indoor flat event. The runners were selected by separate time trials. Billy didn't make it.

There was to be a similar contest later, for which William was still physical training. He wanted to run the same distance for practice. Billy said he would pace him for competition. He took the outside of the track for all curves to give William every chance to make the distance in good time, leading him as long as possible, but expecting William to pass before the end. William never caught up; Billy made a strong finish and "jogged" another lap at the end.

Although William was a strong hurdler and not a middle distance runner, he was a fine athlete, and Billy was very encouraged.

Sweet Briar College, perhaps because of its attractive appearance, or perhaps the social prominence of its board of directors, had from the first attracted daughters of rather prominent families. It was also not long before it got the reputation of having unusually attractive girls. Billy had always enjoyed coming home for weekends. He soon began to know more of the girls.

Since his early childhood, he had hardly known any girls. At VES there were only boys. At Sweet Briar, one of the little girls he had known at his mother's school had fallen victim to polio, and two other girls had left. Other than his sister, there were no other girls there. The university was not yet coed. Billy was unprepared for the masses of girls he began to see at Sweet Briar. On weekends, it was like an enchanted garden peopled by strange and incomprehensible beauties. Billy was completely bewitched.

There was one girl in particular of whom he was terrified, but whose image wouldn't leave his mind. When he could, he watched her from a distance. He had no idea how to cope with this vision.

There was a leap-year dance every Saturday evening in the gymnasium. One Saturday evening before the dance, Billy went to a fashion show, which the girls were giving. Billy's dream girl was modeling pajamas. Her blonde hair and slim, only slightly voluptuous figure, simply drove him wild.

Billy found out her name was Mercer Jackson and also that she was a friend of Lucy Harrison Miller, a girl from Lynchburg whom he had known slightly for a long time. He also found out something, which for him was lethal. She was not only attractive, but was a nice, considerate, well brought up girl. This devastated him. Before he even met her, he had fallen so in love he thought he would die.

One Sunday, Lucy Harrison had a small party in Lynchburg and invited Billy. Mercer was there, so Lucy Harrison introduced them. Billy, while trembling, managed to get into a conversation. He told her all about the architectural school, about the track team, and even about the time he finished the race with the entire stadium encouraging him. When they were interrupted, he confided to Lucy his thrill. She told him to go ahead and ask her for a date. He went outside for a breath of fresh air to steady his nerves, and then, with super bravery and only the slightest squeak

in his voice, asked her for a date. She was perfectly agreeable, but was busy for the next three weekends. For the
fourth, she thought it would be lovely.

Billy had the happiest of months, in spite of a gnaw-
ing feeling that his fraternity wasn't good enough to invite
her to, if she ever came up to the university. She would
inevitably know members of St. Anthony and Deak.

He trained still harder at track, and worked fervently
at his architecture.

The fourth weekend finally arrived, and Billy, quite
happy, yet anxious, made his way to the college buildings,
and sent the maid for Mercer. There was a lovely parlor—
the limit of penetration for beaux. Luckily, the parlor was
empty. In reasonable time, Mercer appeared. Billy's excitement and joy were explosive. All the unhappy moods of
the year were balanced by his present euphoria. All the
creativity of his nature arose to help him express many
things about an array of highly pleasing subjects. She
thought he was perfectly great.

However, Billy once again had to wait several weeks
before another date.

Billy threw his heart and soul into his architecture
and athletics. For the first time in his life, he was completely happy.

His running was going extremely well. There were team
tryouts, which, unfortunately, Billy had to miss. There was
one important meet on the same Saturday of his date with
Mercer. At this meet, three universities vied for honors.
Billy, though nervous, was optimistic and confident. Unknown to him was a varsity runner who had missed the
tryouts. He was listed at the bottom of the team. Each team
was giving all of its members a chance to compete. In Billy's
event, the quarter-mile, there were so many runners that

there were three rows of starters. Billy had the inside track of the third row. The track was not divided into separate lanes.

After the pistol was fired, the runners instantly converged. Two runners in front of Billy collided and fell. Billy jumped over them and continued, but was slightly delayed by the incident. The runners ahead that had not been involved were strung out along the track.

Billy, in the peak of condition, started passing them. When they reached the back stretch, there were only three runners ahead. The third of these runners was one of the stars of his team. Billy was getting closer, but was still five feet behind at the finish. He was fourth, but in a triangular meet this scored one point. Since he had started in the third tier, this was a great victory.

After the meet, Billy had a ride with a pleasant acquaintance to Sweet Briar. They chatted about many things. Finally, his friend asked who his date was at Sweet Briar. Billy said, rather proudly, "Mercer."

His friend announced, "She's very attractive." Then, he added thoughtfully, "I'll bet you have a lot of competition."

Billy, exhausted, but still euphoric after his victory, simply collapsed emotionally. He had been thinking of her as *his* girl. Raised on Sir Walter Scott, the idea of having to compete with others instead of almost worshipping her and enjoying her company, was like a kick in the teeth. His mood changed suddenly from euphoria to extreme depression.

Once again, he returned to the parlor in Mercer's dormitory. He tried hard to be amusing, but it simply didn't work. She tried to cheer him up, but it was uphill going. By the end of the evening, she thought he was simply being grumpy and didn't like it. She told him she wouldn't see him the next day.

Billy understood he was somewhat manic-depressive,

and had long ago found out that when his bad moods came, there wasn't much he could do about it. This time all he could do was hurt, hurt, hurt.

Billy decided to put his best energy into writing her a note of apology. He received no answer. He was neither sophisticated nor self-confident enough to send flowers and try again. He remembered that terrible evening and was miserable.

Later in the spring, William Cabell told Billy he had bought an old Model T Ford at an auction for practically nothing. He invited Billy for a ride during which he told him he had joined the St. Anthony fraternity. Billy sincerely congratulated him. St. Anthony was the fraternity they had considered to be the best.

Back at his own fraternity, Billy was talking to Sterling, and happened to mention William's joining St. Anthony. This inspired Sterling to then reveal to Billy a little previous history. "When you and William got bids from this fraternity, what they really wanted was William. They thought there would be more of a chance he would accept if they also invited you. You accepted and William didn't."

Billy recalled that Sterling, a son of a nice Georgia family, had welcomed him very hospitably, but that the other member of the bidding committee, who was from New Jersey, had simply looked glum.

Since Billy's disaster with Mercer, he had gone through the usual things, including losing his appetite. He was no longer doing well at track. His major spring project, designing a school chapel, interested him greatly, but due to his feelings about Mercer, he had trouble finishing on time. He was no longer able to put enough care and work on the diagram of the building section and received a poor mark on the entire project. He was thoroughly depressed.

CHAPTER 6

Of all the professors with whom Billy came into contact, by far the most notable was his history professor, Springfellow Barr. His modern European history class was so popular that it was divided into two sections. Mr. Barr, a former Rhodes Scholar and a lover and imitator of Oxford, had the ability to make the Reformation or the French Revolution as fascinating as Peyton Place.

He had strong ideas about education. His favorite class, a tiny one, he ran and taught as he thought it really should be done. It met only once a week, in the evening, at his home. He came as close as possible to letting the students teach it themselves. Each would read a paper. The others would discuss it. Mr. Barr would enter the discussion on an equal basis with the students. After about three hours of this, he would leave the room, and soon come back with cider and ginger snap cookies for everyone.

A bright friend of Billy's, Brooke Maury, was taking the class. Billy still needed one more nonprofessional elective unit toward graduation. Brooke persuaded him to try for Mr. Barr's class for the next year, then persuaded Mr. Barr to admit him as one of the five.

The subject matter was the French Revolution and Napoleon. Billy was supposed to parallel the political history with the developments in the arts. He had developed, along with architecture, a deep interest in the history of art. It also happened that at meals he had sat at the table with several other alumni of VES, all older than himself. One of them, Catesby Toulieferro, an unusually bright student, was a seventeenth- and eighteenth-century buff, particularly enthusiastic about their arts and architecture. Billy had begun to pick this up. Hayden, Mozart, Handel, and Velasquez became great heroes to him. He found Mr. Barr's class a wonderful outlet for his feelings. In the first term, he tied the highest grade ever made in the class.

Mr. Barr became interested in Billy. He had seldom before seen such interest in the arts, both past and present.

The Barrs lived in an attractive, small house. A visitor first opened a gate in a high brick wall and entered a small paved courtyard with flowers and vines planted against the inside of the wall. This led to the front door and was also open to the lawn. After class, when the five students were leaving, they frequently stayed there a few minutes chatting with Mr. Barr. One evening, Mr. Barr detained Billy a short while. "You seem unusually interested in art. Maybe you should become an artist."

This unlocked hidden dreams of Billy's, and, greatly flattered by this attention, he expressed interest. He told Mr. Barr he would like to give it thought and discuss it further. Mr. Barr suggested that Billy wait for him in the library the next day and, "When I get out of my C-3 class, I'll pick you up there and we will go down to the Faculty Club and have a long talk."

Like many other brilliant people, Mr. Barr had an unusual philosophy. At a time when there was a fantastic national business boom (1929), an unprecedented stock market advance, and widespread wild euphoria in general,

Mr. Barr simply hated business. He was sometimes called a medievalist: the things of the spirit and the mind in his view far outweighed the almighty dollar. He made constant fun of the workaholic and dollar-chasing captains of industry. His hatred of business development in the world knew no bounds. He sometimes discoursed voluminously on the evils of spending one's life jiggling numbers as an accountant, or putting the same part in a Ford car over and over again as the assembly line passed. He thought businessmen had absolutely no regard for individual people. What he considered to be a mystic philosophy in parts of India intrigued him. He even half defended burning widows in India. He was no friend of preparing college students to make their way in a business world.

Mr. Barr had been a brilliant student himself. He had followed his own tastes and talents, and it had been his salvation. He didn't realize that he himself was unusual; his way of life wouldn't suit most people.

Billy and Mr. Barr made their way down the beautiful sod lawn to that sanctum sanctorum, the highly respected Faculty Club. Mr. Barr, an enthusiastic person, was now enthusiastic about launching a possible new great artist. He would write letters to friends in the art world in New York; he would see that Billy got into the Art League.

Billy, having been constantly unhappy and down in the dumps about Mercer, found the idea of becoming an artist a glimpse of salvation. Mrs. Cabell, whom he admired, liked and respected highly, took occasion to try to steer him back to architecture. William, Sr. wrote him two letters trying to bring him back to his senses. Numerous acquaintances made fun of the art idea, but to Billy they now seemed to be crass, unimaginative dullards.

There was, however, another side to the coin. Billy

found himself becoming tense, forgetful, and having difficulty concentrating. The former depressed spells were nothing compared to what he frequently felt now. He couldn't
shake the artist idea out of his mind. He was having trouble
with his classes; his grades were tumbling. He was late
with his paper for Mr. Barr's class more than once. He
unknowingly overdrew his bank account.

Mr. Barr happened to mention a new biography of
Vincent van Gogh, and suggested that Billy read it. It actually horrified Billy, and greatly increased his depression.

Billy still couldn't quite escape what seemed the glit-
ter of the art career and his real love of painting, and the
arts in general, and go back to what now seemed the pro-
saic and unhappy life he had been leading. He wrote his
father a final letter saying he simply had to go the painting
route.

William received the letter and hoped it would say that
Billy had reconsidered his plan to drop architecture. It
didn't.

William came home early from the office. He was alone.
Natalie had gone to Lynchburg for the afternoon. He sat
down to read the *New York Times*, but he couldn't keep his
mind on it. He remembered his own early struggle in the
still economically disadvantaged South, the hope and excitement of his very few years out West, how his brother,
an excellent doctor in Lynchburg, had found him an ideal
wife, Natalie. He had married Natalie and they had been
radiantly happy.

Then, Natalie had become pregnant. Their carefree fling
was over. Their little cottage was 150 miles from the nearest railroad, and not far from an Indian reservation, the
Wind River Shoshone-Arapaho. Natalie would not consider
the idea of bringing up the child in the wilds of Wyoming.

A letter from Clayton sealed the fate of their life in the West.

The family who had owned the beautiful Sweet Briar estate near Lynchburg had lost their only child and heir, a teenage girl, Daisy, and in their grief had left their entire land and fortune to found a young ladies' college. Clayton had been their executor, and it was now his privilege and duty to create the college. He had already picked the members of the board, and selected a prominent Boston architect, Ralph Adams Cramm, to design the buildings. He invited William to come back East and be the business manager and treasurer. It was assumed the college would grow, and William's job along with it. The offer was just too good. William could do nothing but accept.

In his heart, however, it had been a bad wrench. His sense of duty and kindly disposition wouldn't let him demand that Natalie keep her marriage vow to "love, honor and obey," and raise the child a Westerner. Both of them had grown up with the feeling that no one was really a gentleman or lady without a Southern background or training.

So Natalie left first, per Western fashion, well protected by the stagecoach driver during the several days trip to the railroad.

William had done his best at Sweet Briar. The college had grown and was beginning to prosper. The finances were sound, the buildings and grounds looked beautiful. The place had a fine reputation.

William was on the vestry of the Amherst Episcopal Church. He had always donated what he thought he should to the church. He had tried successfully to keep up the moral tone of the workers at Sweet Briar.

However, William had never really been happy at Sweet Briar. As he sat alone in the living room, it came to him that there was something wrong. He had done all of these things, but the days of his happiness at home had gradually faded. Long gone were those dips in the lake with Natalie as were those 30-degrees-below-zero Wyoming nights when their cottage was warm and cozy. In Sweet Briar, they were comfortable, but it was like a stab wound to realize how he had, little by little, become more withdrawn at home. And his son, for whom he had made so many financial sacrifices, and now realized he hardly knew, was selling his future for tinsel and toys.

Billy's art career began in July at a seaside town in New England: Provincetown, Mass. The entrepreneur of the class was a very famous, elderly artist, Charles Hawthorne, trying to enhance his already good earnings. The classes were actually taught on the beach by a fine instructor. "Spots of color" were the hyped things. The painting was mainly done with palette knives. The idea was to teach the new artists to "see things big," and to get the large, important things in the picture before becoming involved with petty details. Billy thought this was interesting and hoped it might have long-term benefits.

Previously, he had done everything in his work as well as he could and achieved good results. Here, the object was to paint a picture of a model in one morning, using mainly broad knife strokes, and to try for a certain strong effect, but without trying to make anything the least bit fine. "Work big" became almost a religion in this portrait of "Heads on the Beach."

One morning, toward the end of the summer, Billy played hooky from the class and painted a picture of two boats near the beach. Charles Hawthorne happened by in his car and stopped to watch. He liked the picture and praised the speed with which Billy had learned to do this.

The other would-be painters started calling him the genius of the class.

In spite of the droves of tourists and the mosquitoes, Billy enjoyed the two months in the rather pretty small town, but he was not really proud of anything he had done. Even the work of Charles Hawthorne, one of the good portrait artists of the time, didn't really seem satisfying to him, at least not worth putting one's whole life into. What he really liked in architecture and painting was the work of Michaelangelo, da Vinci, and Raphael. The "Heads on the Beach" and even Charles Hawthorne's work were not even in the running.

An artist's ball was a tradition in this art community. Back at the university, Billy had made his own costume for the Beaux Arts Ball. The theme was the "Time of the Crusades." To go as Richard the Lionhearted he had made a suit of chain-linked armor by attaching small cardboard squares to a suit of long underwear and painting them black, a mitered helmet of cardboard, and a shield of very heavy cardboard with the Plantagenet arms painted on it. He received the prize for the most original costume, and his picture appeared in the *New York Times* rotogravure.

For this ball, however, he had no idea for a costume. At the Grey Inn where he stayed, there was no lack of talent; guests included a professor of architecture from the Midwest named La Force Bailey, a recent architectural school graduate, several art students, and Yvonne Twining who was the head student of Billy's painting class. Yvonne decided that Billy must go as a wooden soldier. A borrowed black, long-sleeved jersey with large red paper buttons sewn on, white duck pants with red tape stripes on the sides, black patent leather shoes, and a plain cylinder hat of shiny black plastic with a white bottle brush attached in front as a plume—Yvonne, with considerable help, assembled all this the evening before the ball. The professor of architecture, La Force Bailey, accustomed to doing the make-up for the theater at his college, got Billy heavily made up just before the ball.

Billy escorted Yvonne, who was quite attractive. She had been doing various small art related jobs for pocket money, one of which was to color, letter, etc., several maps of the area, which were to be the prizes at the ball.

At the end of the ball, everyone in costume paraded around the room before the judges. There was little doubt who would get the prize. Billy, resplendent in his flashy costume and make-up, outshone all others, particularly Yvonne, who had spent little time on her own costume. His prize was a large beautiful map of the area, made by Yvonne.

After the ball, there was the inevitable beach party. It was a beautiful moonlit night, made more so by wisps of fog and by phosphorous in the water, which left glittering specs on the beach and in the water for a few moments after a wave broke. Billy was enjoying the company of Yvonne and had moved away from the others. He suspected there was some "skinny-dipping" going on, but couldn't be sure as it was very dark.

At the end of the summer, Billy arranged to go part of the way home by a small coastal ship. It was another beautiful moonlit night, which inspired him to burst into poetry:

> "See the moonlight on the ocean.
> Hear the bell buoy's distant sound.
> See the phosphorous mark the motion
> Of the surf's insistent pound.
> Feel the fever that forever
> Moves our life to show its fire,

See the space of world that never
Reaches end of man's desire."

Billy had arranged to go to the Art Students League in New York for the fall, winter, and spring. He had enjoyed his summer at the seashore, but his ardor for becoming a painter was beginning to sag. He had begun to realize that most of the artists he had seen were not for him. In fact, he was still going on his nerve when he entered the Art Students League for his first class. A quotation he had heard somewhere kept intruding his mind: "Leave hope behind all ye who enter here."

Billy did very well in the primary drawing courses, but in oil painting he had his troubles. Even mixing the colors and simply handling the paints didn't come naturally to him. His first attempts were a travesty. As the winter wore on, Billy became increasingly unhappy and discouraged. He had very little money. Even his attempts to date Yvonne on a low budget were a failure. From time to time, he played hooky from school and went to the Metropolitan Museum of Art. The early Persian display, the Japanese screens, and the entire Renaissance collection fascinated him. He could not reconcile the paintings at the Art Students League with them. To Billy, those in school simply didn't have it.

Painting in a way he didn't completely like was not helping Billy feel enthusiastic. Sometimes he became interested in a picture and did it well, but he was usually "going against the grain" and not getting the best results. He realized that the really great artists had started when they were young children. Early in the spring, he reached the right decision: he was simply wasting money. He would quit. So he returned to Sweet Briar; for the moment he felt himself a miserable failure.

Meanwhile, Polly Cary's career had been fabulous. She

had graduated from Sweet Briar with Honors in Psychology and her mind on an advertising career. At that time, there were few women in advertising. Her search for a job had turned up almost nothing. The only encouragement was from an excellent store in Richmond, Virginia, which, after examining her scholastic record, said that if she would prove her seriousness by working as a salesgirl for eight months, they would try her in their advertising department. She accepted. Sometime before the eight months were over, they relented, and she began to do well in advertising. It soon happened that she read an article somewhere about women in advertising and, on impulse, wrote to the author, a young woman. To her surprise, Polly Cary received an answer. The young lady became interested in her case and offered to help her find a job in New York. This was successful, and she was soon in the advertising department of a major department store, Stern Brothers. She climbed in this position, and persuaded the management to let her open a "College Shop." This succeeded, and soon Polly Cary also added a "Débutante Shop"—both of these within the large, medium- to high-quality store.

The appropriate thing for Billy might have been to try for a job in architecture, but there simply were none. The Great Depression had closed most of the architects' offices, and those still open were laying off their men. The Roosevelt administration was providing aid for the legions of unemployed architects.

In Lynchburg, there was a government subsidized building under construction: a market and armory. The contractor was a family friend, "Chuck" Lewis. He gave Billy a job there as a carpenter's helper, 7 a.m. to 5:30 p.m., four days a week, and 7 a.m. to 7 p.m., two days a week, all for $12.50 a week. In addition, Billy had to walk almost a half-mile there in the morning and back in the evening. For the first few days, he could hardly make it, but then he began to prosper mightily.

The hard labor was a complete physiological rest. Billy gained weight and took pride in his ability to finish the seven o'clock evenings in good shape and then walk home. He stayed at his uncle Robert Massie's home where the food was the "old Virginia" type.

Billy admired the steel workers who climbed like squirrels all over the structural steel. He watched as they would heat bolts red hot, then pick them up with tongs and throw them 20 or 30 feet to the place they were needed, where someone would catch them in something like a large funnel. They would then be put into place while still semi-plastic, and their ends became flat enough to make a sure lock. Once in a while they would miss, and heaven help anyone below.

Billy was determined to learn to walk the high steel beams. His first tries on low narrow beams were a success. Then he was to deliver some bolts to men at the other end of a higher beam. He managed to get half the distance in good shape; however, there was a power shovel working immediately beneath him. This confused him, and he lost his nerve. He froze. There was nothing he could hold onto; if he fell he would land on the power shovel.

The three steel workers, at the end of the beam, saw him and thought it was very funny, but it was only seconds until one was out to assist him to a large vertical steel column, which he could hold onto. Billy regained his composure. He returned to terra ferma by some other route.

This job had started during the cold months, but finally, spring was around the corner. Billy could now walk the high steel beams. One of the carpenters with whom he was friendly said, "Come here, I've something to show you." They walked the steel beams to the end of the building. "Look at that, isn't that one of the prettiest things you've ever seen?" It was a grass field on a hill top, beyond the river, emerald green in the spring sunshine. Billy readily agreed.

Later that day, Billy was lower in the building, pulling nails from a forming board for reuse. Everett Fauber, a former excellent student at the university's architectural school, a fellow member of the Scarab fraternity, and a former roommate of Lawrence Anderson, came by to see him. "I'm leaving in two weeks to study architecture in Europe by the 'travel and sketch method;' Why don't you come with me? We will meet Andy in Paris, travel with him through northern Europe as far as Stockholm, then head back as far as Vienna. We'll later go back to Paris via Munich for a week or two, then travel down through Italy and go to Greece. It will be a trip we'll never forget; and we'll learn more about good architecture by actually seeing it than by reading about it in books."

Billy was sorely tempted. He had a certain sum of money from an inheritance. It would be enough for the trip. The exchange rate for the dollar was very high; in some of the European countries one could live or travel for what seemed almost nothing.

Once again, Billy made the right decision having agreed to go. Years later, he realized that this trip provided education, which was extremely helpful to his career.

At this time, there was a happy event in the Dew family—Polly Cary's marriage.

For several years, she had been dating a young chemical engineer, Bill Woodson, and had finally agreed to marry him. Everyone liked him. He was doing beautifully as head production engineer in a U.S. Rubber plant (and making almost as much money as Polly Cary at that time).

The wedding was in the Episcopal Church in Amherst. There were several parties, the most beautiful being Meta Glass's in the stately old house in the beautiful garden. Immediately after dinner, it was arranged that everyone gather in the large hallway at the bottom of the stairway. Suddenly, music played from above, and the entire Sweet Briar choir came singing down the stairs. The two leaders were beautiful freshmen. One of these, Bonnie Wood, made quite an impression, particularly on Billy.

CHAPTER 7

Billy's trip to Europe was a great thrill from the start. He took a passenger freight ship to Le Havre for about 10 days, each of which were very much enjoyed. Professionally, however, things were quite slow in starting. Paris was hot and humid. The Louvre was not well arranged and was poorly lit. At Versailles, neither the palace nor the gardens were well kept.

Notre Dame and the Sainte Chappelle were fascinating; Billy simply loved them.

Everett, it turned out, soon made friends with the American students at the Ecole des Beaux Arts, and was having a pleasant time, but had no great interest in the architectural monuments or the famous works of art to be seen in and around Paris. They spent several days in Fontainebleau where there was an American school. They lived only a block away from Louis XIII's palace, and only Billy bothered to go through it. This also seemed true of most of the American students there. They were having a great time, but weren't really doing much that they wouldn't have been doing in the U.S.A.

Andy, whose three-year scholarship required and financed extensive travel, was away when Billy and Everett arrived in Paris. When he returned, things started improving

drastically. They soon started their trip through northern
Europe. Andy had the greatest appreciation for everything
good: the buildings, the museums, the old villages, the
gardens, the restaurants. He was even a connoisseur of
the wines. Billy was beginning to profit from the trip, as
well as enjoy it immensely.

The modern movement in architecture was gaining
ground in Europe. One automobile showroom in Paris was
almost all glass and quite attractive. The Van Nelle factory
in Holland was the first really good looking and interesting factory Billy had ever seen. In Hilversum, all the buildings were designed by the same architect and supposed to
be great milestones of the "new era": the town hall, the
slaughter house, the bath house, and more, all good looking, and renowned. The only trouble, Billy thought, was
that they all had towers and looked very much alike.

The young men had what, for them, was a unique experience. Billy had German family connections who were
quite prominent in Bremen. He remembered his aunt had,
for years and years, corresponded with them. Billy could
remember his aunt's German husband, John, who was very
kind to him, but who had died when Billy was still a small
child. He had built a tobacco factory in Lynchburg and
married Billy's aunt, Sally, who was one of the prettiest
girls in town. The factory had been prosperous, but was
ruined by the American Tobacco Company, the owner of
which had offered to buy the factory at a fair price. Wilhelm
had refused to sell and had been run out of business.

Billy's aunt still corresponded with his family in
Bremen. He knew they had a son, Wilhelm, around his
age, and made arrangements to meet him in Bremen as
they passed through. Billy and his friends met him at his
office at "one half five," and they spent the rest of the

evening with him and a friend of his. The evening included wine at the Rathaus and dinner at a fine old Bremen restaurant.

Stockholm was wonderful with its beautiful blonde girls, its Town Hall and Carl Milles' sculpture. The archipelago was most impressive passing a goodly number of speedboats, many with blonde girls who waved as they floated by.

Vienna was also wonderful. By pure luck, while they were getting a ticket to the various important buildings, it happened that the head of the town council was in the same room for a moment. He engaged the young men in conversation, was interested in their trip, told them he was just starting out to drive an important visitor around Vienna, and that they might come along if they so desired.

This drive was extremely interesting and a great education since they heard the political and business side of both the new and old construction. This was something that had not happened to them before.

The Schönbrunn garden and palace in Vienna were particularly intriguing. Not since Versailles had they seen anything like it.

Billy and Andy, the most enthusiastic of the group, in addition to seeing Europe's best art and architecture, were getting an even improving sense of periods and styles. In museums, they made a game of trying to correctly guess the painters, the country of origin, and if possible, the approximate date of paintings or sculpture, before getting close enough to read the title block. The winner would likely be the first to discover and identify a room full of Rubens, where acres and acres of canvas, painted by Rubens himself and/or helpers were very easily identified. This game could not be easily played with buildings, since they usually knew what they were before seeing them.

The boys were lucky to see all of these things before World War II. The old buildings of Belgium and Holland; many things in Germany, particularly the Frauenkirchen; and many things near it in Nürnberg and Dresden, were damaged or destroyed in the war.

After Munich, the young men went to Nürnberg, and, as the last stop, Rottenberg. Andy was returning to Paris to complete a project at the Ecole; Everett had met a girl there. Billy particularly liked Rottenberg, and decided to stay there two or three days, then go to Venice via Munich, stay there a week, visit Verona, Vicenza, and Bologna, and meet Everett in Florence on October 8th.

Billy's first day in Rottenberg was cloudy, with a little rain. He went up on top of the town wall, right over the main gates of the town, with a view up the narrow, curving main street, looking up toward the apparent cathedral, to paint a watercolor. The dull, slightly rainy day, the leaden colors, the dull red roof tiles, and the beautiful, double-ended Gothic church, seemed to him to express the soul of an age long gone.

That afternoon the weather improved and Billy set out over the woods and fields to a nearby hamlet to see a charming, very small and simple Gothic church with a famous altar piece by Riemenschneider, one of the best wood carvers ever. The completely unspoiled rolling countryside, the tiny, old hamlet, and the church with this marvelous altar piece, provided one of Billy's most fascinating afternoons.

That evening, Billy enjoyed another great stroke of incredible luck. Beginning to feel a little lonely, he went to a nice looking weinstube for dinner. While enjoying a beer and waiting for his dinner, he happened to notice a fine looking young man on the other side of the room who seemed to be looking at him. The man somehow looked familiar. In a few minutes, he got up and came over to Billy's table. It was Wilhelm, whom Billy had met in Bremen, and who was, with a friend, driving through Bavaria in his Ford roadster for his vacation. They had several more days to go and invited Billy to join them.

These young men were not only pleasant companions, but were highly educated and savvy on the affairs and politics of Germany. They first headed for Dinkelsbühl, a small town which had, like Rottenberg, been ruined by Gustavus Adolphus in or about the seventeenth century, and had hardly changed a timber since.

Soon after breakfast their first morning there, the young men were standing in front of their inn, enjoying the view of the town in the morning light. A number of cars, obviously an organized motorcade, drove up and parked in front of the town hall a short distance away. They were ostensibly advertising "Deutschland Gewaken" (Awakened Germany) cigarettes. Singers and a small band performed a stirring song. Wilhelm told Billy it was the Nazi hymn, "The Horst Wessellied." He also said the cigarettes were only a front; it was really a Nazi rally. He warned, "Hitler is not good."

After a few more days in the beautiful country and old towns of Bavaria, they arrived in Munich from whence Wilhelm was to depart for Bremen. Hans was to drive the car back separately, stopping at his old university en route.

Wilhelm spoke English quite well; Hans did not. Most of the conversation during the trip was either in German or in English between Billy and Wilhelm. On the street in Munich, they fell into a serious conversation in German. At the end, Wilhelm said to Billy, "I have to go back to Bremen to my office, but Hans does not. If you would like, Hans will continue to drive with you and see more of Bavaria." Billy was enchanted.

For the first half hour, they drove in complete silence, as Billy spoke no German and Hans no English. Suddenly, a rabbit ran across the road. "Da, einer hase," exclaimed Hans. It was no problem for Billy to understand this. With the few German words Billy had known for a long time, a little imagination, and Hans' pocket German-English dictionary, they began conversing. Granted, in the evenings, the hotel clerks would have to translate between them to settle any problems of plans for the next day, but Billy was rapidly picking up German.

For Billy's education, as well as pleasure, this trip was glorious. Hans had always wanted to see more of Bavaria. He, highly educated in German art history, knew where to find the best rococo, Romanesque, gothic, and whatever else Bavaria had to offer. They even visited Neweschwanstein: an exquisite and still unspoiled site right on a deep blue lake, a most interesting and superficially beautiful monument to a mad king and a ponderous, confused era.

Much of the best rococo in Europe was in Bavaria. It simply dazzled the eyes. As something to look at a few times, it was simply glorious. There was also the Romanesque in the Rhine Valley. Hans staked a claim that it was the best in the world, ahead of the French. One afternoon they stopped by the Graf Zeppelin hanger on Lake Constance. The Zeppelin was there. It was an extremely impressive sight. Once they went to the origin of the Danube and saw the little marble temple with a large brook running past it. Then they went to the schloss of the Fürst von Fürstenberg, a fine, somewhat small palace, with a famous collection of illuminated manuscripts.

Finally, Billy's friend Hans had to leave for Bremen. Billy continued down the Rhine to Cologne, then by rail back to Munich, stopping off at several towns along the way. The Octoberfest was just beginning, but he avoided it and took the train to Venice right through the Alps.

At 12:00, Billy took his eyes off the mountains and pushed all the way up to the dining car. He couldn't get in; they were about to cross the border into Austria. He went all the way back to his car, and duly opened his bag for the Austrian border police. He enjoyed Brennero and then once more started for the dining car. The same thing happened, as now they were approaching the Italian border. He went all the way back and once again opened his bag for the Italian police. Immediately after the border, he tried again. By this time it was getting late, and he was very hungry.

Billy happened to strike up a conversation with a most attractive couple there. The gentleman owned a dump truck factory in Munich, and she was from San Francisco. They were interested in Billy's trip, and he stayed a long time talking with them. Once more, he walked all the way back to his car. There was no car there! This was a disaster, as Billy had left all of his traveler's checks in his suitcase. He had only a few dollars in his pocket.

Billy went for the conductor, who said the car had been transferred to another train, which was bound for Vienna. At the next stop, Bolsano, the conductor and Billy raced several blocks to the telegraph station and sent a wire to the police on the border to intercept the suitcase. The American Express office in Venice was helpful and immediately wrote a letter in German to the border guards, not to the American consul's office. They typed out a long document canceling Billy's traveler's checks, and only charged him a small fee, but were of no more help. Apparently, he could live or die as far as they were concerned.

Billy signed up to stay at a small pensione (boarding house) just behind the St. Marco Basilica. This was easy to find: just go past the Basilica on the left, cross the bridge, go one block, cross another bridge, turn to the right and go a few feet, and there it was. Billy signed up for a week— they didn't know he had no money.

Every morning he would go to the American Express office and inquire about his bag. For the first four mornings, it was not there. Meanwhile, life went on. Billy discovered an Italian wine he liked very much: Gancia Bianca. He limited himself to one small glass of it per day, which he would get at a small bar on the west side of the Piazza San Pietro. His meals were at the pensione.

Finally, one morning at the American Express office, Billy's bag appeared. Everything he had in it was there, but in a different place than he had put it. Evidently, the police had searched it well. He immediately cashed a travelers check, went back to the consulate, and completed payment on the document. This time he was well received. The young man he had talked to there was now the soul of courtesy and invited him to have coffee in the Piazza San Pietro just outside their office.

Venice, beautiful Venice—the world's most beautiful city. Billy now had his sketch pad and colors and used them every day. He wanted to see everything there, walking through the streets and campos. At one church, which he considered one of the best looking in town, he remained until the afternoon when people began to enter. There was obviously some ceremony taking place. He couldn't figure out what. He simply found a good seat and watched, without understanding a word that was said.

Much later on, friends suggested that it was simply a vesper's service. He never found out for sure.

Billy also took a boat trip to the islands of Murano, Burano, and Torcello, and another to the Lido. On Murano, he saw the wonderful old glassmaking plant.

Verona was another nice town. Billy made a watercolor of the famous bridge, then years later made another, much larger oil painting of it. It also had the most beautiful Roman arena he had ever seen.

In Bologna, the address he had was evidently to a former great house, which was still beautiful and beautifully maintained. The food was quite good, as was the service. The other guests were nice looking; he wished he knew them. He became all the more anxious to learn Italian.

On October 8th, Billy arrived in Florence. First stop— the American Express Co. There were two letters there from Everett. The first said, "Everything is fine. See you in Florence on the 8th. The second said, "I've had a bad flu attack and gone home to the States."

Billy felt marooned, six thousand miles from home. He knew not a single soul in Italy and hardly knew anyone in Europe except his friends in Bremen. That evening, he really learned what loneliness was.

This lasted until 9 o'clock the next morning. He asked the management of his little pensione what to see first in Florence. They immediately said the church of Santa Croce. It wasn't far, so Billy started on foot. Before he had gone two blocks, he simply fell in love with Florence. There were no great monuments on the way, but almost every building, every statue, and everything else he saw was perfectly proportioned and beautiful in conception and detail.

The inside of Santa Croce was almost in itself a history of the Renaissance. In fact, in its paintings and sculpture, it was the closest thing to the *Bible* that lay people could use to understand their religion. The *Bible* in Latin was only usable for the clergy and intelligentia.

Santa Croce was also a virtual history of Renaissance art, from the very early paintings made and shaded with almost pure, extremely thin gold, through the primitives; one masterpiece depicted Mary Magdalene washing the feet of Jesus, while various devils were exorcised from her. Billy was delighted that in one beautiful primitive of angels bringing good tidings to the shepherds, one angel flew low while the shepherd struggled to keep his dog from barking at it.

Across the interior courtyard was a Michaelangelo/Brunelleschi masterpiece, the Medici chapel. In the nave of the main church were a goodly number of tombs of the great and famous—beautiful examples of Renaissance sculpture.

The night before, Billy had what seemed to be a major bad break. That morning he had a lucky good one. While he was drinking in the charm of the main nave of the complex of related buildings, he was astonished to see a horse in armor led in through the front door, accompanied by a group of men in armor and in twelfth-century costumes. There was also a priest, who sprinkled holy water on the horse. There was evidently a ceremony in progress. Billy picked an inconspicuous spot and watched in awe.

Billy finally found out that this was a yearly ritual in honor of the general's horse, which had saved the general, and enabled him to win the battle and the war against Pisa in or about the twelfth century. (Pisa never completely recovered from this. Its only big asset was now its tower, which brings in millions of dollars a year, because a mistake in its footings almost 900 years before permitted it to lean, which makes it one of the world's premier tourist attractions. Never mind that the tower, the church, and the baptistery form one of the most beautiful architectural achievements in Italy, or in the world.)

Billy was soon able to get a permit to sketch in the Uffizi gallery. One morning, he was making a monotone sketch of Raphael's "Goldfinch Madonna." Various groups of people came by while being lectured to by professional guides, who were obviously repeating over and over again the gallery's position regarding the greatness of the arts therein. Soon, it happened that a well-dressed, prosperous-looking group came, being lectured to by a distinguished-looking man whose views were obviously his own. He was berating Perugino, one of whose masterpieces was hanging nearby: "Perfect in color, perfect in composition, completely lacking in inspiration." Billy was fascinated by this and started following the group and listening. Soon, an attractive lady approached him. "This is my group. The members pay handsomely for these lectures by Tealdo Tealdi. However, I can see you are probably a student, and really interested. I sometimes let students audit these lectures. If you would like, you may do so. All you will have to do is write me a letter later on and send me one of your sketches."

Billy was not about to miss this opportunity. Tealdi was an Oxford-educated Florentine who had held various important posts in Florence, among them Curator of the Davanzati Palace. Twice each week, he took a group of enthusiasts to important museums or monuments in Florence. His comments on history, art, politics, and general conditions in Tuscany, and even Europe in general, formed much of the basis for Billy's thinking. The lecture "Bernini and the Baroque" formed a linchpin of his concept of architectural history. The end of the most beautiful part of

the Renaissance and the growth of the impusle toward
power at the expense of proportion, order, and thoughtful
design were the focus of Tealdi's lecture. Not that Bernini
wasn't good; he was very good. His sculpture portrait of
Louis Quatorze, his Piazza San Pietro, and many other
things were proof of his talent. The great period of the Renaissance was ending; the buildings, paintings, and sculpture became more wild looking, less beautifully proportioned, as if striving too hard to make an impression.

Billy believed the great Michaelangelo's work on the
Sistine Chapel's west wall (completed many years later)
was powerful, forbidding, and intended to evoke fear—further evidence of the end of the Renaissance period. Gone
was the great charm of the ceiling. Billy thought the figure
of Christ more powerful physically than spiritually. (Was
this Michaelangelo's fault or that of his boss, the Pope?)
Martin Luther had hung his theses on the door at
Wittenberg, and many people in central Europe were following his lead. Henry VIII had rebelled from the Pope.
Venice had always been a problem. The armies of Philip II
of Spain, under the Duke of Alba, had defeated the Pope's
own army and captured Rome, the Duke having fallen on
his knees before the Pope asking for forgiveness for fight-
ing him.

Billy thought he would never want to leave Florence,
but he decided, after almost three months, he should continue his trip. Next came Siena, with its gold background
pictures and a beautiful cathedral on a stunning site. It
was probably just as well that the Palio wasn't being run
just then; but Billy enjoyed the stories about it.

Next came Orvieto, formerly the great Etruscan town,
with its black-and-white layered cathedral.

The American architectural students in Europe usually

stayed in more or less the same places, and, in those days, got their mail and their financing at the American Express Company. This was fortunate. It meant that they all met each other. At Billy's *pensione* in Rome one morning, just as he was getting up, there was a knock at the door, and in came Ralph Ellefret, and another student, Johny Chimales. They were both on traveling architectural fellowships and were soon going to continue their trip through Naples to Greece. Billy had, by now, toured Rome fairly thoroughly. He had been several times to the Vatican museum and one or two others, which he thought outstanding. He had tried to learn every detail of the Sistine Chapel, not only the magnificent ceiling, but also the wonderful frescoes and the architectural details on the walls. He noted that most tourists came in, looked at the ceiling, and paid little attention to the architecture of the room, the screen, the mosaic floor, and, above all, the frescoes on the wall, which were done by a very small number of the greatest painters of the Renaissance.

Billy decided he liked his new friends and accepted their invitation to go along with them to Greece. He fell ill in Naples and left a week after them. This may have been fortunate. To save money, Billy's friends decided to go deck class from Brindisi to Piraeus (the port of Athens). On this small ship, this meant they had a choice of places to sleep: either the deck or the freight hold. There was a fairly severe storm. The hold was crammed with all sorts of things, including a number of pigs. As the storm got worse, the pigs became seasick and threw up all over the floor. Although the hold was down in the hull, there was a very large door in the side for loading the freight. This was less than water tight. As more water splashed in around the door, it became harder to dodge the mixture of salt water and pig vomit that swept from side to side in the hold as the small ship rolled and pitched.

CHAPTER 8

There was wet snow falling when Billy left Naples. As the train reached higher country inland, the snow grew deeper. It was a pretty trip through Bari to Brindisi.

The next morning, Billy cleared legal formalities and carried his bags to the docks. There were two small ships there, both with names clearly visible, but written in Greek. This was a rough beginning for him in understanding things in Greek. He finally succeeded in deciding which one was the Adriaticos.

Due to Billy's recent case of what someone had called Neapolitan fever, he thought he should go in a fashion more deluxe than his friends had, namely, second class. That, he found out, meant sleeping in a room with several peasant men, and also eating at a large table with a number of them. Not many passengers or crew could speak English or French, but in so far as they could communicate, about all they seemed interested in was how much money he had with him. At nights, he slept with his wallet and traveler's checks in an inside pocket with a suede jacket zipped up tightly outside of it.

The small ship had a large funnel, and around it, perhaps to protect it in a serious storm, there was a metal partition. Inside of this, it was nice and warm. This area seemed to constitute the social center of the second-class and deck passengers. To pass the time, Billy practiced his French with a few seemingly reasonable men who said they were returning to Greece from the University of Paris. He later realized his mistake.

The trip was beautiful. After a short stop in Albania, early in the morning, came Corfu, with time to go ashore and explore. Then, around sunset that evening, Billy was speaking in French with a nice looking young man from first class. He suddenly noticed the ship was going along near a high cliff. He then looked to the other side, and there was another. The young man answered his query as to what it was by what sounded like "Itheike." It evidently was Ithaca, the long ago home of Odysseus of the Trojan war stories. Billy was fascinated.

That night the ship docked in Patras. It was announced that there had been a landslide in the Corinth canal, and they would have to go around the Pelaponesis to Pyraous, the Port of Athens. The next morning, they cruised down the coast past the snow-covered mountains near Olympia to the island of Zante. After Zante, the sea grew more beautiful, with seemingly clear green water with purple streaks, and from time to time many small islands. Billy remembered the stories from Greek mythology he had heard when he was a small child. These islands might have harbored anything from the Sirens to Polyphemus, particularly with the unreal look the storm and spray gave them.

However, early in the day his friends' from second class, who apparently thought all Americans were rich, had conceived the idea of "share the wealth," in the form of a loan from him. They were growing more persistent. Billy began to grow scared. He decided, for safety sake, to finish the trip first class. He went into the first class office to make arrangements. There was no one who could speak any language Billy could speak. The outlook wasn't good.

He had previously noticed, however, and exchanged words with, a large and athletic-looking young man from California. He seemed to be a nice person and was, like Billy, making a European trip, currently en route to meet friends in Athens. Billy hunted him down and engaged him in some interesting conversation. He stuck with him and refused to speak anything but English to anyone else. These two Americans together completely discouraged the French speakers.

Billy's two friends had left Athens when he arrived. He spent two wonderful days in the museums. He sketched the famous 4,000-year-old Minoan "lion" dagger and jewelry, and a beautiful classic Greek wine casque. The second day, he was able to make a satisfactory drawing of a nude statue.

On the third day, Billy's friends returned from southern Greece. Johnny, who spoke Greek very well, had gone all the way to the bottom of the Pelaponesis, and had stories of donkey trips through the rugged mountains, and little known old Greek remains. Ralph had stayed in Sparta.

The Acropolis generated the usual fascination. The three young men saw it by day and by moonlight. There was only one light, a bare bulb, apparently about 40 watts, near the entrance stairway. They made watercolors of it, sketched fragments in the little museum just east of the Parthenon, studied the very perfect, tiny Ionic temple of Athena Nike, and in general, with the greatest enjoyment, took advantage of this rare opportunity.

The young men also, of course, walked to the top of Mt. Licabettus, on the walkway lined with century plants, some of which were in bloom. One afternoon, they even climbed Mt. Hymettus.

A little later they spent more than a week in Mikonos, which was, at that time, completely unspoiled. Their reservation was at a tiny hotel, the only one on the island. They signed up at 35 drachmas a day, full pension. The drachma was 180 to the dollar.

As soon as they got settled in their room, hardly believing the low rate, Johnny went back down to verify it. He carefully concealed that he spoke very good modern Greek. He briefly discussed (in French) a few casual subjects, and then said in an off-hand manner, "Let's see, our rate is 35 drachmas each..."

The patron said, "No, that isn't right." Johnny prepared to argue. The patron continued, "Your rate is 20 drachmas a day."

Johnny, astonished, hung around, pretending to examine the picture on the wall. The patron was conversing with another Greek, and Johnny heard him say, "I quoted these kids 35 drachmas a day, but that really wasn't right, so I'm letting them have it for my regular charge, 20. They're nice kids, and they'll eat several cakes every day, which are extra, that's enough."

Mikonos then fully deserved its fame. It was defined by very narrow winding streets with small houses, all flat roofed, all mainly white, with brightly colored doors and windows, painted a clear, pretty, light blue or green. Many houses had small exterior stairs to the second floor, the first floor being some kind of shop or work area. There were almost as many tiny churches as homes. Along the edges of the town, stood many white windmills with thatched roofs. Mikonos was a wonderful place to create watercolors.

Billy found out there was another tiny town on the other side of the island: Enumera. It was only 8 or 10 kilometers away. He wanted to see it. The other two thought it too far away. Early Sunday afternoon, Billy, alone, began to trek.

To his surprise, the central part of the island was almost a desert. He was walking on a road, which was simply a track made smooth by occasional use. There was no sign of human habitation anywhere. The day was a little cloudy and the scene seemed spooky. Billy heard the faint sound of hoof beats, the source of which was unknown. Once again, he remembered his Greek mythology. Some little inner voice was whispering that they might be a Minotaur or even a Gorgon.

Finally, Billy's path carried him to the summit of a small dune; the hoof beats also reached one. It was a peasant riding a donkey. A few dunes later, the donkey caught up with him. The peasant addressed him in Greek dialect. Billy wasn't able to understand one word of his dialogue. The peasant grew more excited. Finally, he dismounted and lifted Billy onto his donkey. He had been offering him a ride. Billy had somehow picked up the Greek word for "Thanks." It came in handy.

So, he rode into Enumera in style. It was a pleasant Sunday afternoon and most of the townspeople were in the square. Enumera, it seemed, was at least as sophisticated as Mickenos. The village square was beautiful. As Billy dismounted, a friendly crowd gathered around him. Someone who was able to make him understand in some language, apparently acting as their spokesman, asked why he had come to Enumera. Billy was stumped. He couldn't think of an answer that would make them understand. In the nick of time, he spotted an intriguing, perhaps sixteenth-century, small church, on an adjoining side of the square, and said, "I've come to see the church." The crowd immediately parted and formed an avenue for him to walk through to it. Several children proceeded him into it. They ran around the nave, kissing several icons as they passed, and then left. It was beautiful. Billy stayed as long as he thought he could. The crowd was still there. Their emissary invited him to a tavern on the square.

Inside, it was almost like a scene from "Never on Sunday." They were drinking wine and singing Greek songs. Billy was fascinated. He enjoyed the wine. Also served were absolutely delicious small fish. There was someone at his table who had been a WWI prisoner of war in Germany and who had learned a little German. Billy succeeded in talking to him. He almost hated to leave. Also, having recently been in Paris and recalling stories of people being hideously swindled, he dreaded what his bill might be. He was very, wrong. "There is no bill, you are our guest," he was told by the proprietor.

With much handshaking, and sort of a guard of honor for one block to the edge of town, Billy started his trek back.

In Mikonos, it was Karnival time, just before the start of Lent. Billy's small hotel had the largest room in town. It also had what seemed to be a never-ending party. It lasted three nights.

The hotel kept turning back the clock before Lent and provided a great band for the festivities. The band played old Greek tunes, as Greek folk dancers performed. Billy and his friends participated, or endeavored to do so.

A pretty Greek girl, named Irene, was there. Billy had become acquainted with a Turkish archaeologist who could speak both French and Greek, and, before the end of the party, Billy persuaded the Turk to introduce him to her.

Irene spoke nothing but Greek. Billy shook hands with her, but that was the end of that.

The next evening Irene was nowhere to be found. Billy asked the archaeologist where she was. "Irene isn't here, but her brother is." The brother was standing there, ready to fight. Moral: Don't make advances toward Cyclades Island native girls, except through family members and unless ready to propose matrimony.

Míkonos was only a very short distance from Delos, the presumed birthplace of Apollo. The young men found out that there was a fishing boat that frequently carried supplies there, although there seemed to be only one inhabitant. They engaged a passage.

There was a dramatic avenue of archaic lions in fairly good shape. Opposite it, there had been an equal avenue of phallic symbols. One or two were left intact, but most were in pieces. It was understood that two missionaries of a conservative and not well educated American church (which shall remain nameless here), had smashed all the rest. The young men were told that an ancient Greek cult had worshipped the penis as the giver of life.

Other architectural remains were of interest, particularly a wall with a lion gate, which structurally approached the principles of an arch.

Back in Míkonos, Billy greatly admired the many small churches. They were simple and beautifully proportioned. Inside, many had handsome screens separating the little naves from an area at the altar. One in particular the young men sometimes called the "cathedral." It may have been over 40 feet long over all, and was probably the largest and most handsome in the village. It even had a small, beautifully made ornament at the peak of the front gable where Western churches might have had a steeple. Inside, it was also simple, but it had perhaps the most beautiful screen on the island.

A very small plaza, perhaps 60 feet-by-60 feet in front, reached to the edge of the harbor. One afternoon, Billy set up his little folding stool close to the water and made a watercolor of the church. A good breeze blew a little spray on him from time to time. The sketch turned out well. Years later, it was a fine decoration in the office of William B. Dew, Jr. A.I.A., Architect.

The young men enjoyed another deck class voyage from Piraeus to Catania, Sicily. They bribed the concierge to let them sleep in second class. Upon landing, they received a very practical lesson in finance. They had turned in all their drachmas in Athens and, after the above mentioned necessary expenses on the small ship, had practically no immediate cash left. They would immediately cash traveler's checks for lire in Catania.

They were told, however, "The United States has closed all its banks. There is a world financial crisis. We can't cash your checks."

The young men couldn't even buy lunch. However, others from the ship had also come to the American Express office. A nice Scotch lady remembered them, and seeing their plight, proffered a loan of five lire, with which they were able to eke out lunch. They already had reservations for the night.

The next morning things improved. The people at the American Express office said America had made guarantees, which enabled them to cash the checks. The young men went to a good restaurant, had a wonderful lunch, repaid the five lire debt and (after proving to their benefactress that they were really proffering a silver 5 lire coin and not a 20 centesimo coin, which resembled it) caught the train for Taormina.

Not only was Taormina reputed as one of the most beautiful spots in the world, but the train trip up the east coast of Sicily was unforgettable. A beautiful sea on one side, Mt. Etna, snow-capped, rising above fields of orange trees in full bloom, on the other.

Most memorable in Sicily were the mosaic ceilings in the churches in Monraeli and Cefalù. The only catch to this was that the young men could not possibly hope to do anything like this back in the States. In miniature, though, maybe it could be approached, if they were lucky.

Because of financial restraints, the young men were doing Europe "the hard way." They detrained early in the morning in Anzio, checked their bags there, and with necessary clothing, etc., in knapsacks, walked to Amalfi. The walk was as beautiful as expected. Then two days later, they walked to Positano, which they simply loved. While they were lunching at a very simpatico tiny restaurant, it became obvious that a storm was threatening. A number of the typical brightly colored and patterned boats were on the nearby beach. The fisherman owners were beginning to pull them up farther from the waves. The young men enjoyed greatly the novelty of assisting them.

Those who had given or were administrators of the traveling fellowships, which were providing these trips for Ralph and Johnny, had wisely allowed for extracurricular activities like these. It was felt that visiting Míkonos, Enumera, Positano, Rottenberg, Dinkelsbühl, etc., improved the young men's taste, and gave them a sense of town planning. These things were a fine foil for the large museums and great buildings.

The young students had an unusual address in Assisi. There was a convent there which, when founded in the thirteenth century, had as its mission assistance to travelers, who were, in those days, mainly pilgrims to Assissi. This was still its purpose. Through Catholic connections in Chicago, Johnny had heard of it and made arrangements to stay there.

The main central room was impressive: large, vaulted, with two fireplaces. They had their meals there on a handsome, long, heavy table, with the mother superior as hostess, sitting at the head. The food and wine was exceptional. The comfortable living quarters opened from that, on the opposite side from the entrance to the convent. They were not exposed to any of the young novitiates.

The mother superior was cultured, caring, and understanding. This was a great experience for the young men. Unfortunately, the trio broke up at this point. Johnny was going straight home; Ralph was going to Vienna; and Billy to Spain.

Ralph had planned a bicycle trip from Bolsano to Vienna. Billy was extremely anxious to join him in it, but he had to see Spain. Soon, he received a letter from Ralph: "My father got panicky at the local financial news—everything in the States seemed falling apart. He told me to drop all plans and come home immediately. The next morning, I took the train to Paris—right through southern Germany and the Rhine valley, without a stop."

Barcelona, Tarragona, Valencia all had something memorable for Billy, particularly Barcellona: a plus for the Rambler, a minus for the new Cathedral. Cordorba, made him sad with hardly more than the mosquito left of its long-ago glory as the Moorish capital of Spain.

Seville seemed to him the soul of Spain with the beautiful cathedral, the Patio de los Naranjos, the Giralda (a melange of Moorish and baroque), the gardens, the roses, the Casa de Pilatos, the Plaza de Toros, and the Feria de

Sevilla. Billy's lodging was on Amor de Dios (Love of God) Street. Ray Stirton, another traveling architectural student, whom he met at the American Express office, lived on Jesus Street. Together, they went to the quintesential Spanish sport, the Corrida de Toros (Bullfight). Billy had heard of a place (Pamplona) where the bulls were turned loose in the street before the main event, and the braver pedestrians were to run amongst them. He couldn't remember where this was. Possibly it was right here. They decided they didn't feel brave, so they went very early for avoidance. This was lucky, because they simply loved the seventeenth-century arena. They forgot the bulls and examined it with the greatest care.

The opening of the bullfight season on Easter Sunday was a huge event in Andelusia. The music, the ceremony, the gorgeous costumes, the extreme skill, and incredible grace of the participants, the adulation or extreme condemnation of the spectators, simply thrilled Billy and his friend.

The best talent in Spain and Portugal was there on the sand. First, two bulls came in the Portuguese way, then the matadors on beautiful white horses. They were not supposed to kill the bull. After the usual foreplay (apparently to excite the bulls and perhaps tire them slightly, and to give the lesser grade performers a chance to exhibit their skill and bravery), came the climax of the act: the matadors, after certain maneuvering, with incredible skill, came ever so close to the bull's horns. They then reached over them, stuck darts in the bull's shoulder, and rode. This was all done with the greatest bravery and grace and incredible horsemanship. Billy and his friend saw this done twice, and still could not possibly understand how they were able to do it.

After these acts, came six bulls in the age-old traditional Spanish way. First, the magnificent bulls came charging into the arena. The *capas*, in silver, crimson-lined capes, at first were to run from the bull to encourage it. There were certain places in the periphery of the arena, where they could slip through to shelter, but the bull couldn't. With Spanish style, the object was to let the bull come as close as possible before escaping. After a little of this, they would taunt the bull with the crimson cape linings, and display their courage to the utmost.

Next came the *banderilleros*, who further taunted the bull and finally maneuvered right in front of it, and, over its horns, stuck the *bandas* in its shoulders.

Billy understood that all this was not only to entertain the spectators with a further show of grace and bravery, but to further tire and confuse the bull.

Next came the act, the *picadores*, which most foreigners, particularly Americans, could not forgive, and which Billy considered an example of the worst trait of the Spanish: tolerance of cruelty. *Picadores* dressed in a certain amount of armor, and with strong lances tipped with sharp *picos* (points), came out on blindfolded horses. It was assumed that the bull would attack the horses. The picador was to defend them with the lance. Sometimes he could, and sometimes he couldn't. One or two of the horses were killed by the bulls. In this case, it was a further duty of the capas to distract the bull and save the picador.

Next came the final act. The matador, in the most expensive and magnificent of costumes, and with the greatest grace, appeared to the thunderous applause of the audience. He had a sword and a medium-size, blood-red cloth, which he frequently draped over it. He taunted the bull, but was at first supported by the *capas*. This enabled him to work up to his act while studying the bull, and perhaps somewhat confusing it, as well as entertaining the audience. Finally, the *capas* retired to the sidelines, leaving only the bull and the matador, but staying ready to distract the bull with their capes in case they had to save the matador's life.

The matador would then put on a fantastic show of courage and skill, confusing the bull, perhaps lying down momentarily, turning his back on the bull, draping his red cloth over the sword and encouraging the bull to charge it—all manner of things to show his superiority over the furious animal. Through all this the matador was also finding out how the bull would react and whether he would come for the flag or for the man. He was frequently very close to the bull. Finally, when he sensed the time had arrived, having gotten the bull's attention fixed on the flag, he would, over the bull's horns, plunge his sword deep into the animal's shoulder in such a way as to, if successful, produce an instant kill.

Easter Sunday had drawn the best matadors in Spain. To kill the bull was far from the entire object. Each matador had his own deeds of grace, skill, and courage to perform first. A great deal of the program was almost in part a ballet to the beat of the *paso doble*. A matador's Spanish style displayed while working the bull was as important as his skill at the final sword thrust over the angry beast's horns.

The Easter bullfight was not without special thrills. On that day, a matador's presumed final sword thrust did, as frequently happened, pierce the bull's shoulder. But a sudden muscular movement of the bull dislodged it, and it flew end over end into the air, then hit and stuck into a bench just between two spectators.

One of the matadors made an awkward movement and
the bull's horns pierced his middle. Billy and his friend
were aghast as the bull tossed the still impaled man and
shook him from side to side in the few seconds before several brave *capas* distracted it with their capes.

While walking home to Amor de Dios Street and Jesus
Street, Billy and friend felt they had received their initia-
tion to Spain.

South Spain seemed to cast a spell over Billy—the
gardens, the roses, the ironwork, the narrow winding
streets with softly colored houses, the tile work, the paintings. Most of these things were purely Spanish, and could
not easily be reproduced in the U.S.A., but, nevertheless,
Billy thought they were broadening his architectural vo-
cabulary. He did some of his best watercolors there. One
was of a simpatico patio, entered through a beautiful old
wrought-iron gate. One day, two very well behaved small
children were watching him paint and he put them in the
picture, exactly where the composition needed them. Another time, a peacock perched on a tile bench and then
proceeded to strut around as if posing. Billy caught it in a
very quick action watercolor.

The *Patio de los Naranjos* at the cathedral fascinated
him. The mixture of water, orange trees, and the tiny ca-
nals to carry away the waste water from the fountains were
intriguing. Billy later found the same things in other places,
including the beautiful Alhambra. He made a careful, detailed sketch of the central fountain.

Madrid seemed a bustling, mainly nineteenth-century
town, and a big let-down from Audalusia. Redeeming fea-
tures were Billy's pension and the Prado Museum. In the
Galician pension, the patron, with the consideration and
hospitality, which Billy had frequently noticed in Spain,

gave him an individual small table at meals, and asked one of his other paying guests to sit with him for company, and to help him with his Spanish and his understanding of Spain. As a typically Spanish gesture, this friend very soon brought Billy a gift, a paper backed book titled "*Los Caballeros las Preferen Rubias*" ("Gentlemen Prefer Blondes"). Billy very soon succeeded in reading it.

Billy simply fell in love with the Prado Museum, particularly the Velazquezs: *Las Meninas* and *La Rendicion de Breda*. Farther down a long room were Goya's *La Maja Desnuda* (La Maja nude) and *La Maja Vestida* (La Maja clothed). Down another long room were some of the best of El Greco.

In the Plaza Major, there were, mercifully, few traces of the sixteenth century Inquisition. The history of the *auto-da-fé* was sickening. It was for students a frightening example of religion run amok. Billy couldn't help noticing that in most countries of Europe, the church had permitted or carried out many horrible executions: the Albigensian Crusades, the murders after the revocation of the edict of Nantes, and many others. One of the worst was the burning of Joan of Arc. He refrained though from siding with a friend who said, "The Church was one of the worst terrorist organizations in history." The art of the old masters showed many scenes of terrorist crimes against the Christian martyrs, but very few were recorded of the church's own violence against those who incurred its wrath.

Billy sat alone at an outdoor table at the Cafe des Deux Magots in Paris, where he had been many times the previous year. This was long before the existentialists had made it so very famous. On this, his last evening in Europe, he had time to reflect on his wonderful trip. Or so he thought. He viewed a familiar face, that of Archer Jones, whom he remembered well from the university. Archer was a star basketball player, a member of the great DKE fraternity, the son of a family of the elite of Richmond, the city in the state with the most tradition and the greatest history in Virginia. Archer had been one of the five in Mr. Barr's history class and the leading one until, in a fit of indecision, he resigned.

Billy and Everett had seen him several times the year before. They had also enjoyed meeting his mistress, an unusually beautiful Swedish artist's model, not to mention the pleasure of seeing several nude paintings of her at the spring salon.

Archer was alone and joined Billy. He said he was broke and asked Billy to buy him a drink. Billy obliged, but warned that one was all he could afford to do, as he had figured his French cash to the last centime—one taxi ride to the train, breakfast the next morning, every tip, every possible expense. (Actually, Billy's father, who was now financing his trip by sending payments from his own bank account and had been very late in sending one, so that a large part of the last payment had gone to pay debts already made. Billy had barely enough left to get to his ship. He already had his train ticket and his transatlantic passage. Other than this, he was completely out of francs.)

Archer wanted to be a writer. He said he had been working hard at it. Almost nothing had sold. He regularly received a small amount from a trust. Whatever cash he had, he mainly left at home for fear he would spend it.

Billy told him about his trip, which was now ending. Archer asked how all these wonderful things he had seen would help him practice architecture.

"That remains to be seen. I can't believe that seeing, studying in detail, and inwardly digesting these great things won't help me. Back at the university and other places in the country, I frequently heard mention of Palladio, the Renaissance, the Roman style, Regency, etc., but usually by people who didn't really know very much about them. To really experience styles such as these was bound to help. I realize we were going into modern style. We saw that too. Seeing and studying the world's best architecture and gardens day after day had to help. It gave one an idea of what buildings could look like."

Archer said he enjoyed living a bohemian life in Paris, but he was now getting sick of it. He had thought that this would teach him more about life and help his writing. He had taken this course because he couldn't stand the idea of tying himself up in an office somewhere for the rest of his life. Archer made one last request: that Billy lend him the metro fare home. He lived in Montmartre, and they were now on the left bank, half a city away. Billy felt very bad, but simply couldn't do it. They said good night, and Archer started a very long walk.

Billy thought, "If I hadn't mercifully come back to architecture, there might I go."

CHAPTER 9

America was still mired deep in the Depression. There were no jobs to be had in architecture. No one knew how long the Depression would last.

Henry Dew, in Florida, was vice president of a major holding company, the Almours Securities Company, and at that time, co-receiver of a bankrupt chain of hotels. He had invited Billy to come to Florida, and would, as soon as possible, get him a job with his company's strong firm of architects, Marsh and Saxilby. This firm now had not a single thing to do. In the meanwhile, he would get him "something."

The "something" turned out to be assistant relief clerk in a small commercial hotel in West Palm Beach, the Dixie Court, at room and board and $7.25 a week.

West Palm Beach was simply the service entrance to Palm Beach, a famous mecca for the extremely rich and famous. The Dixie Court was the best out of two small hotels open in the summer in West Palm Beach. The building was fairly new and not unattractive, with the inevitable pecky cypress paneled lobby and tiled floors. The manager was suspicious that Henry had sent Billy to ultimately take his job from him and was interested in seeing that he did not succeed. Simply staying there and acting as desk clerk, during the slack time of day, was not Billy's dish. He became depressed. He was interested, however, in exploring Palm Beach, easily reached by a good bridge.

There had been a flamboyant and successful architect in Palm Beach, Addison Meizner, who had built a number of large and expensive houses in various and exotic styles. This was during the Florida boom. When the boom collapsed and his socially prominent angel, Paris Singer, who had been getting him jobs, had become angry with him, his practice also collapsed, and he had sought greener pastures elsewhere.

At this time, there were several architects there who were still seeking out practices. One of these, Maurice Fatio, foreign born, handsome, and exuding continental charm, was doing extremely well. His clients were so well off that the Depression had not hurt them seriously. Several of his jobs had turned out beautifully.

In the era when some of the top titles in England were financing themselves by marrying rich American young women, it befell that some of these marriages were disasters. The bride in one of the marriages, Consuela Vanderbilt, who had married the Duke of Marlboro, had finally obtained a divorce, married a handsome French officer, and moved to Palm Beach. Fatio was building them a small palace.

Billy went to Fatio's office and applied for a job. They seemed to consider him, based on some of the drawings and watercolors he had made in Europe, but said they really did not need anyone else.

Billy also visited two other architects, but with no luck. The one that came closest was Volk and Maas. Billy pondered this, and after checking it with William, wrote them a letter offering to start work at $1.00 per day. They accepted.

The Dixie Court manager, delighted to be rid of what he considered a threat, allowed him to stay there at cost. William provided a little support.

Billy gave himself a small vacation between jobs, and returned to Sweet Briar for a few days.

Natalie, anxious to see Billy married, and regretful of his distaste for the church, tried to kill two birds with one stone. Bonny Wood, who had made such a hit with the male members of Polly Cary's wedding, was also a leading member of the Sweet Briar choir, and prominent in whatever church activities there were. Bonny was also a talented dancer, and not only beautiful, but graceful in every movement. She was also a very good student and had won the Mason Scholarship, which Clayton Manson had bequeathed to the college

During Billy's stay, Natalie invited Bonny to Sunday dinner. Billy was duly fascinated. Somewhat later, Natalie sent Billy pictures of the May Day celebration at Sweet Briar. Bonny had narrowly missed being May Queen. Her best friend, Peggy Carey, a fine looking girl, but not nearly as pretty as Bonny, was very rich, a great athlete, a great personality, quite popular, and a power on the campus. It was she who organized Bonny's campaign for May Queen. Bonny was far prettier than the winner, but not as popular. She easily won second place: maid of honor.

Early during the winter, Billy went to Palm Beach, applied at Treanor and Fatio, and made it. Fatio's office was on beautiful, large Phipp's Plaza, very near the center of Palm Beach, and opening off its principal north/south road. It was paved only with its own road, which ran around its periphery. The rest was well watered lawn, with flowering shrubs, small decorative trees, and a huge banyan tree near the middle.

On his first day at Fatio's office, the chief designer had to go to one of the handsomest houses in Palm Beach and took Billy along to help make measurements. It was not one that Fatio had designed; it was Arabian style, not really suitable to Palm Beach, but very attractive. With a large internal courtyard and fountain, and much of it on one story, it seemed to Billy a very simplified and smaller Alhambra. Fatio had only been called in to make minor adjustments. They went through most of it. This was a great opportunity for Billy. He saw how a beautiful foreign style had been successfully adapted to suit a rich American.

A further opportunity was in store. Besides the former duchess, there was another important client, this one from the American Midwest. His house was now well under construction, but Billy was assigned the detailing of bathrooms and closets. This was really the best looking house done by the office that year. Billy became very familiar with it.

The government of Palm Beach practically worshipped the "tourists"—the term they used for the people who came down from the North in the winter, and who provided the prosperity of the local businesses. There was a town ordinance against any construction after late autumn so as not to have any loud hammering, drilling or even any truck driving to disturb them. A quiet, beautiful town was the object.

This affected the architects there in that anything to be built had to have plans ready by at least late summer and for any major projects much earlier still. After that, there was not much work for them. The offices were down to only their chief designers by the start of the "Season."

This also meant that the hours of work were very long, and the pressure deadly during the spring and summer.

The employees did not complain because they had to make a year's supply of money then.

The first part of Billy's work day ran from nine to five, with an hour for lunch. He usually had dinner somewhere in Palm Beach and came back to work around six-thirty or seven. He was home by 10 or 11.

He was able to find a job with a small, though not very good, architect in Miami during the winter. By early spring, he was back with Fatio.

Due to the small number of budding architects wanting to go as far south as Palm Beach in the summer for a half-year's work, and the resulting heavy work load, it was quite a strain. Palm Beach was beautiful in the summer, with everything green from the constant showers and flowers or flowering shrubs everywhere. The hottest days weren't nearly as bad as those in, say, New York, but the heat was constant and damp.

By July, Billy didn't feel well. By September, he was ill. The doctor, backed up by a second opinion, diagnosed it as a rather rare tropical fever brought on by Billy's still low resistance to disease and by his long work hours. Six months rest was prescribed. There was nothing to do but go home to Sweet Briar. To make it much worse, Billy, having always been bothered by weak eyes, had strained them badly with the long hours of close work combined with the brilliant sunshine during the day. The ophthalmologist diagnosed it as acute eyestrain and advised Billy not to try to continue with architecture.

Just resting at Sweet Briar was excessively boring. As Billy began to strengthen and improve, he began to feel more the lack of any younger people around. Most of the professors there were much older, married, and tied down by their home life and profession. Mr. Worthington had a son a little younger than Billy, but who was quite retarded. There was one young language instructor, Clarence Houston, who seemed peculiar and who fell unreasonably, yet understandably and unrequitedly, in love with a less than blazingly attractive student. Nevertheless, Clarence provided some companionship when Billy was able to become more active. However, these people paled in significance beside another happening.

Bonnie Wood, now an alumna, came back for a weekend visit. Natalie found out she was there, told her Billy was sick, and asked her to come down to see him. Bonnie was much obliged to the Dew family since the scholarship she had received had been created and financed by Natalie's brother, and so she was glad to come.

Billy, bored, depressed, and idle, was completely captured. He had no thoughts for anything or anyone but Bonnie. To make it worse, Natalie found out that Peggy Carey, who had rented a house only two miles away, would be there for at least a year working on a certain forestry project in memory of a brother who had been killed in WWI, and that Bonnie would be her assistant.

The girls lived in a small house more or less in the woods between Sweet Briar and Amherst. They also had a small barn and two horses, which they rode almost every day. Billy also discovered that they usually came over to Sweet Briar daily for their mail. They were almost always together.

Billy, while improving, was still the victim of forced inactivity. He could think of various ways to see them, but most, such as ride with them, take them to the movies in Lynchburg, offer to guide them in exploring the adjacent hills, streams and forests in connection with their project, were still beyond him physically.

Natalie had several beautiful flower beds. One morning, Billy picked a very large bowlful of several kinds of flowers and took them to the girls. The flowers seemed well received. Billy very happily stayed a short while until the girls said they had some errand to do and then drove home with a feeling of success.

Billy had now found that he could frequently encounter them at the little college post office or the commissary or the book shop and at least have a nice chat with them. Sometimes, he could even bring them down to his home for some refreshment such as a Coca-Cola, but there was a problem: they were always together, so he could never get Bonny alone.

From time to time, the effluent Peggy was visited by various presentable suitors; Bonny never was. The two girls seemed happy as they were.

There was a certain amount of social life on the Sweet Briar campus. The head of the athletic department, a strong red-headed woman, who was a former Phi Beta Kappa in college with an enthusiastic and agreeable personality; a professor of English, also red headed; and a history professor, all occupied an attractive small house, which had been designed by the college architect. There was also a secretary who commuted from Lynchburg and who liked fast cars and gambling on the stock market. These people formed the nucleus of a manless society. None had an alcohol problem, but none failed to enjoy a good drink. The head of the athletic department was sometimes alleged to smoke cigars. Peggy, who was accustomed to a fun social life, and Bonny, who followed her, became junior members of the group.

Some half-mile away, across the hills and streams, in the opposite direction from the lake and mountains, was a large and handsome house, originally built by the sister of the owner of Sweet Briar plantation. It was in findesiecle architecture with many columns and a large porte-cochere and was far from unattractive. It also had beautiful grounds with handsome shrubs. A Mr. Barrow, a well-off Lynchburg manufacturer, and his wife now lived there.

Billy, in spite of the doctor's warning, did not give up entirely on his profession. His eyes began to improve rapidly, and as soon as he could, he began to study for his architectural registration exams. He now had worked the required two years under a registered architect and was qualified to take it. This was a perfect chance to concentrate on his books: history of architecture, general construction, steel, trusses, concrete, general principles of design. He soon found he was enjoying this unexpected opportunity to concentrate on these things. He also realized he was becoming quite adept at them.

As Billy grew stronger, he gradually became more active. He even started hiking a little on some of the old trails. He also found that he could sometimes see the girls while swimming at the lake. The old problem remained, though: how to separate them. In desperation, Billy concocted a scheme. He had formerly had success in making soap carvings and also small statuettes in modeling clay. He would make a bust of Bonny. She would have to pose for it.

First, a little carpentry job: a rough table with a small revolving platform on top to make it easier to view the sculpture from any angle. (It was also realized that this could be used to study architectural details, and Billy was still tempted to spend time on painting and sculpture, even if only as a hobby.)

He was now succeeding on spending more time with the girls on one pretext or another. Peggy was by far the more outgoing one (and really the nicer), but Bonny's face had sunk deep into Billy's heart. She was becoming an obsession with him. Worse, he was losing sleep over her. Finally, he could stand it no longer. He went over to their house when he knew they were there, and said he simply had to talk to Bonny. He told her he was absolutely crazy about her. She showed little interest. She said he would have to get over it. "I like someone else."

Billy left, distraught. He went by to tell his troubles to Clarence. This did no good.

There was another young language teacher, Salvatori Mangiafico, a Sicilian, who was married, outgoing, and far from peculiar. Billy confided in him. Salvatori said he had known Bonny fairly well when she was an undergraduate. He had known that Billy had a very serious crush on her and had prophesied no success. Bonny and Peggy had been fast friends since their freshman year, and in fact, they were practically inseparable. Bonny was the only child of rather poor parents; she was spoiled, petted, unsophisticated, self-centered, bright, and beautiful. Peggy was just the opposite: handsome, strong, outgoing, and sophisticated. She was the daughter of the president of the Pullman Company and so was thoroughly accustomed to an active social life. Further, she was a generous, kind person, well liked by almost everyone.

Billy was raised on Sir Walter Scott, where the deserving hero always gets the beautiful heroine. He had had a limited social life. As a very poor art student in New York, as a traveling student in Europe, and as a beginner in architecture in Palm Beach, there wasn't much money for that. Bonny was simply too attractive. He couldn't get her off his mind.

Polly Cary mercifully invited Billy to visit them in New

Jersey for several weeks, until he had become interested in other things, recovered his composure, and, once again, was able to sleep at night.

CHAPTER 10

It was very easy to get from Polly Cary's home into New York, which was fortunate. It happened that, when in New York several years before, Billy had met a rather successful architect who had mainly a top drawer residential practice and who was a cultured, admirable person. Billy went to see him and discussed his predicament—that it appeared he couldn't continue with his profession because of his eyes. Mr. Houston, now retired, advised him to get into the building supply business, specializing in high-grade products. Billy's architectural experience and talent would give him a large advantage in that business, and he might become interested in it. This gave Billy just what he needed: a new interest. Almost every day, he went into New York to various places which exhibited building products. He became well versed in the industry. (Years later, he realized that this was one of the best things he could have done at this time.)

Upon returning to Sweet Briar, Billy tried to continue his studies by correspondence and in whatever way he could. He found that an acquaintance in Lynchburg, "Sparrow" Goode, had a high-grade building supply company, so he contacted him. Sparrow was very enthusiastic about having Billy join his company.

Billy, however, wanted to "keep one foot on shore." He found that the state examination for architectural certification was to be given in about three months. He would take it and in the meantime study hard for it. He became quite involved in this task. He studied the history of architecture (for which the Europe trip had given him an enormous advantage), design (which he thought depended mainly on natural ability), structural steel, reinforced concrete, trusses. As far as his courses had gone, he became very adept at all of them.

Natalie was still dead-set on Bonny for a daughter-in-law. She did not subscribe to the idea of an overly close friendship between the two girls. Soon after Billy's return, she found out when Bonny would be at Red Top, arranged for her to be alone at a certain time, and sent Billy there on an errand. When he rang the bell, Bonny opened the door. This strategy worked. Billy was enraptured after only one brief conversation with her.

However, Billy realized that he had never gotten the least encouragement from her and that the two girls had seemed happy living together in "the woods." Peggy had beaux visiting her, but Bonny, although beautiful, never had. Billy thought Bonny was probably reveling in the role of being sympathetic to a spurned suitor. He didn't go for it. He decided that he would be polite but just a little mean to her.

The architectural exam was a killer. Four days of testing: eight hours each the first three days and 12 hours the fourth day. The first day covered general engineering. Billy could cope with all of it, but didn't come anywhere near to finishing on time. He didn't think he would possibly get the minimum of 60 percent, which was required on each separate part of it in order to pass the examination. Nevertheless, he continued with the rest of it and, thinking he had nothing to lose, enjoyed it greatly.

The papers were graded almost immediately. The next day he had a surprise: he passed. The number of questions on the first day's work was loaded so as to test the facility of the applicants. It wasn't expected that anyone would finish; it may even have been that Billy was the one who got the most done.

Not long afterwards, Billy saw Mr. Mackielski, who had been on the board grading the papers. Mr. Mackielski, who had taught him "Reinforced Concrete," said his paper was one of the best they had ever gotten.

Billy took a short vacation, then started studying again. This time he studied the line of products carried by his friend's engineering sales company. Actually, this was getting down to the nuts and bolts of building; it was to be the greatest help to him later in life.

Billy's job was mainly to contact people, sometimes people quite far away who had expressed interest in some of the products. Other than that, he was simply a traveling salesman. It might have been thought that Billy's shy, reclusive disposition was completely unsuitable for this work. He began to enjoy it though; he found it exciting to contact possible customers.

One line of products he was pushing was acoustical materials. He had studied hard the science of acoustics initially. One afternoon he called on a potential customer, the principal of a large country high school. The problem at hand was to improve the acoustics in their auditorium. Billy made a good impression. The principal said there was a meeting of the school board after dinner that night and asked him to come back then. So Billy soon found himself making a speech to the school board on the science of acoustics. Actually, this was much more exciting than working as a draftsman in someone else's office. This job was extremely good for Billy. He was going all over a large part of the state learning to deal with people, observing how business really goes on, and seeing a side of life about which he had known nothing.

In the town of Charlottesville, where he had gone to the university, there were five architects, three of whom had been friends of Billy's at the university. They were a great help to him. He also found out, unexpectedly, that he got along very well with the contractors. His previous experience as a "hard hat" on the market and armory building and his friendships with the workmen there seemed to serve as a bond. He soon was doing so well that he opened a branch office of the company he worked for in Charlottesville.

Billy got permission from Goode to take one account himself: a fine variety of stove, the Aga. He soon found himself dealing with the president of the company. He found this exciting.

Billy's eyes and general health now seemed far better. He had been around the state enough and had been exposed to different architects' offices to realize what the profession was really like. He was licensed to practice. He had grown self-confident. He had seen many sets of plans created by several different architects. He thought he could do better. He now had no doubt that he would rather spend his life as an architect rather than a contractor.

The ordinary commercial practice of architecture had little allure. In Palm Beach, Billy had seen the best. Because of his health, he couldn't reasonably try Florida again.

In the northern part of Virginia was a large and beautiful area of manicured countryside with large mountains in view and priceless estates. It was largely devoted to a very glamorous and expensive sport: fox hunting. Billy had heard it called "The Kingdom of the Horse." People in more conservative (and less wealthy) parts of the state considered it wicked: a land of beautiful horses, fast women, and no morals. It was an area settled by Yankees, who had been so hard hit by the Depression that they were not only down to their last yachts, but also were retiring and building palaces in the horse country because during the Depression there were fewer millions to be made in stock brokering.

It happened one day that Billy was in the office of a very nice young architect in Winchester, just on the edge of horse country. An attractive young couple was there getting ideas for their house. The architect had to leave, and he left Billy there to explain his products to them. The temptation was just too great. Billy started telling them how to build their house. It gave him the strangest pleasure.

Billy treated himself to a long drive through the area. He was completely sold. In particular, there was a small town, rich in history, quaint looking, with a goodly number of early nineteenth-century brick or stone houses: Middleburg. This seemed to be the center of the region.

In the center of the town was a large, eighteenth-century inn, now in great disrepair and closed. Its stonework, general look, and simple details, seemed just the right thing to go with the attractive, unspoiled old town.

Billy returned with one thought in mind. He would open his own architectural practice in Middleburg.

Several kind people wrote letters of introduction for Billy. Natalie wrote one to an old friend who invited him to a large party for the more Southern-oriented members of fox-hunting society. One of the most venerated grand dames of the area who had known William as a boy, spoke in a very friendly way to him at the first opportunity.

Another letter was to Mr. Atkinson, a patrician fox hunter with a Southern background. Billy went to see him and presented the letter. He was impressed with Billy's academic record, particularly his study in Europe. He told him the eighteenth-century inn that he had liked so much had been bought by three prominent local people to be remodeled and gave Billy a letter to one of them, Mr. William Stephenson.

Billy wasted no time in presenting it. He also told him that he had been interested in the building on his earlier trip. Mr. Stephenson said they had already hired an architect who had examined the building and reported that it wasn't worth trying to save, and recommended demolishing it and saving the lot as a real estate speculation. Billy almost had a fit, he was so anxious to remodel it. Mr. Stephenson said he had been bitterly disappointed as he had been very anxious to put it in top shape and reopen it as a fox-hunting inn similar to those where he had stayed in the Cotswolds in England. He said he was impressed with Billy's study in Europe. They went down and looked at the inn.

Billy's enthusiasm was obvious. Mr. Stephenson told him to make some sketches of what might be done, and he would give them serious attention. Billy made measurements of the building and started rough sketches. He called Mr. Stephenson and suggested that they go over them together. They were soon creating them together.

Billy found out that Mr. Stephenson was a graduate of Princeton and Oxford, was very bright, had been an enthusiastic fox hunter both there and in England, and was well known among the fox hunting aristocracy.

During the next long planning session, Mr. Stephenson told Billy that Jack Vietor, one of the trio that owned the building, would be at his home for the weekend, and that he would arrange for Billy to meet him.

Jack Vietor was 25 years old, had an enormous after-tax income, was good looking and active. He seemed to spend his time commuting between Palm Beach, Hollywood, Georgetown, and London, as his mood or social events dictated.

Jack thought the Red Fox Tavern a fun project and was all for it.

Actually, the tavern was a fertile field for an architect with a good imagination.

Originally, there had only been a kitchen on the ground story, which, along with the whole story, had a dirt floor. The walls of the kitchen were exposed stonework, and there was an enormous old fireplace, which still had an old iron kettle suspended from an old iron crane. The top of the fireplace was simply an enormous arch, and, over that, a large timber on two handmade wrought-iron brackets served as the mantel. Later, a poor quality concrete slab had been poured on the entire basement. The old kitchen had been cut up into small rooms. The front of the ground floor now sported a drug store, complete with soda fountain, and commercial booths and a small hardware store.

Billy and Mr. Stephenson loved the huge old fireplace and the stone walls. Mr. Stephenson wanted to do what he had seen done in the Cotswolds: have a fire always burning in the fireplace and have a *pot-au-feu* (a stew) always hot and cooking in the iron kettle. He said it would be great to come in, cold and tired from fox hunting, and have a drink and a dish of hot stew and French bread.

There was also an entrance directly to the street. They would take out the flimsy partitions, add a Williamsburg-style bar (as in the Raleigh Tavern) and call this the Tap Room. They would remove the old soda fountain and commercial type booths and make that room, which connected with the bar and also opened right off the street, the dining room. The old hardware store would become the kitchen.

The racing bookie and Boy Scout headquarters upstairs would become the lobby of the inn and be paneled in eighteenth-century style. There would be a small apartment for the manager. The two floors above would be guest bedrooms, each with an added modern bath and nice closets.

The third owner, Mr. George Garrett, a diplomat and stockbroker, was now easily sold on this plan.

One difficult problem persisted. The tap room was heated by wall hung radiators—real eyesores. It needed the heat. Otherwise, Billy felt sure he could give it the Early American appearance they wanted. (Floor heat was still experimental then.) There simply weren't any eighteenth-century radiators.

Finally, Billy thought he had it. He would design rather simple Colonial-style benches with high backs, which would hide the radiators and which, with natural wood finish, would go with the bar. They would appear warm and welcoming and be like the banquettes in many fine restaurants. There would be room behind them for air circulation. The air would come in at the bottom and go out through countersunk brass grilles in the horizontal top.

A bar was a necessity. Billy took great pains to find the smallest beer cellar to be had. With this and a small sink, he succeeded in getting it in. The exterior was of old pine with the panels copied from others in the old building. Some of the boards came from across the street and were donated by Mr. Stephenson. It was said that they had been used in the Civil War as operating tables for wounded soldiers.

Billy was preparing large, finished details of the whole room. Jack Vietor was quite interested and wanted to see the sketches. He invited Billy to come to town (about 45 miles) to have dinner and show them to him.

Jack's place was most attractive. One of the rather small, early Federal-style houses in the elite, fashionable, old part of Georgetown. It had a rear terrace overlooking a simple, but attractive garden. Billy, still in great awe of his client who could make or mar his project on a moment's notice, was led by the butler, Phillips, to the terrace. Jack soon appeared, and started entertaining Billy with his recent adventures in Hollywood. Billy was fascinated but kept his roll of drawings ready. Jack called the butler and ordered two Scotches. More dissertation regarding Palm Beach and Hollywood followed. Finally he said, "Let's look at the drawings."

Billy started unrolling them. The door bell rang. Phillips appeared, guiding a beautiful young lady, a Powers model. The drawings were for the moment forgotten. Once more, Billy was fascinated by the conversation regarding cafe society in New York. The brunette beauty also wanted to know who Billy was, whether he also had a house in Palm Beach, with what pack he fox hunted in Middleburg, and whether he liked the "Patio" in Palm Beach. Billy was bewitched.

Unfortunately, this vision soon said she had only dropped in for a moment and was going to a dinner party. She left.

Jack became eloquent on the subject of the brunette, but finally the conversation showed signs of drifting back to the drawings. Another attractive young lady quickly appeared. Jack said, "Eleanor Flood is going to have dinner with us. Let's wait until after dinner to see the drawings."

More Scotch appeared. Eleanor, the niece of Senator Richard Byrd, was good looking in a calmer way, charming, and obviously much at home in social and political circles in the area. She seemed to consider herself the hostess. She was soon joined by another couple. At almost midnight the party broke up. Jack said, "Oh, I guess we forgot the drawings. It's too late now. Why don't you come in for dinner again tomorrow? We can put more time in on them then."

The next day, Billy, still nervous, was there at exactly the appointed time. Once more, the same thing happened. And a third time the next day. Billy was rapidly getting broken into the rigors of a "society" practice of architecture.

Mr. Stephenson, however, was a different type. He and Billy met almost every day, conferring on the seemingly infinite number of problems, which occur in a project of this kind. The problem of the wall-hung radiators seemed solved. The old, cracked concrete floor in the tap room and dining room had to be removed. The thing these rooms needed would have been wide-board, perhaps pegged flooring. This couldn't be done as there was no way to provide ventilation under it. It would soon have rotted. Once more, the project seemed stalled. A brick floor might have sufficed, but it wouldn't quite have given the rooms the elegance they wanted, and it was alleged that tables would "jiggle" on it. Further, there were numerous other restaurants and bars of greatly inferior caliber, which it would have resembled.

Finally, Mr. Stephenson said he had dinner with Mr. Walter McKay Jones, who lived in a certain house, Ayrshire, said to be the largest in the state. Although retired, Mr. Jones owned a small company which had a patent on a certain substance and process for making floors, which might possibly be just what they needed. Mr. Jones wanted them to have lunch at a well-known restaurant in Washington, O'Donnell's, in which they had installed one of these floors.

Billy knew that Mr. Jones had a Lincoln Continental car, which in those days was regarded as the snappiest of convertibles. Mr. Jones, partially paralyzed, could have no outlet for his energies except driving the car. Billy, a lover of fine cars, was thrilled when Mr. Jones insisted on driving them to the city in the Continental.

The martinis were good at O'Donnells. Mr. Jones and Billy enjoyed each other, since both had fond memories of Spain, particularly Andalusia. Mr. Jones had been all through the Casa de Pilatos, which Billy had not. Billy was now finding that his trip through Europe had not only provided 90 percent of his design education, but was also helping him greatly with his clients.

The floor they had come to see gave great character to this seafood restaurant. It was intended to imitate driftwood, and it succeeded, Mr. Jones thought it could imitate old pine in the Red Fox Tavern.

He sent his sales manager, Mr. C. Huddleston Bear, to see the tavern. Mr. Stephenson and Billy were already sold on the floor. The sales manager wanted to use the identical color they had seen in O'Donnells. Billy and Mr. Stephenson wouldn't have it. The Red Fox Tavern was no place for driftwood. Billy stuck to his point and wouldn't approve it until the sales manager finally agreed and submitted satisfactory samples of a color similar to old pine. Tiny furrows made with a straight edge imitated the cracks between boards. For the pegs, holes were bored and re-filled with the same material colored a little darker. The still-soft material was broom swept in a certain way to imitate wood graining. One had to look very closely to tell that the finished floor was not old pine.

For an office, Billy had rented for practically nothing an old one room building only one block from the Red Fox. In it was a nice old fireplace with a simple, good looking mantel. He had stripped the paint off all the woodwork, which was of beautiful old pine. He had two drafting boards and stools and had bought a kitchen chair.

Jack Vietor had called and said an important lady, Mrs. Lucy Lynn, might want to stay at the tavern when it was finished. He asked if Billy would show it to her the next Sunday afternoon and perhaps plan an apartment especially for her in it.

Mr. Stephenson told him that she, although no longer in or near her twenties, was the glamour girl of the fox-hunting crowd. He said she had been mentioned as one of the 10 best-dressed ladies in America by the society editor of the *New York Times*. He said she had the best horses, the best clothes, and was one of the very best riders of all. He also believed she was the sister of the man whose small palace Billy had helped design in Palm Beach.

That Sunday afternoon Billy came down to his office well in advance of the appointed time. He soon observed this fashion plate (she was in full regalia, just out of a Sunday dinner party) walking up the little hill to his office. Billy helped her off with her beautiful fur coat. He hesitated a moment, as there seemed nowhere in the office to put it. She laughed and said, "Just put it on the floor." She couldn't have been nicer. Billy was enthralled.

She was, indeed, interested in spending the hunting

season at the Tavern. Billy showed her the drawings and the building. They selected three rooms to remodel for a small apartment for her. She had many, many ideas for closets, drawers, coat hangers, and lights. Billy worked all of them into his plan. He enjoyed greatly working with her. He was now finding out that the rich and famous could, after all, be tolerated.

Word about the tavern was spreading through horsedom. Before long, another grande dame, Betty Hubbard, was also interested in future quarters there. Billy also worked with her. Immediately over the tap room was an area that Billy turned into a large bedroom with a fireplace, a bath, and dressing room. It opened both to the rest of the tavern and to the outside. Once again, everything was arranged exactly as she wanted.

Once again, there was a call from Jack. A Mr. Ramon Tartiere was interested in the project. He did not want to move in; he already had a large and beautiful place, Boxwood. He was merely interested in the project and wanted to hear about it. Late one afternoon, Billy took the plans to Boxwood, which had formerly been home to General Billy Mitchell. His Scotch was delicious, and Billy enjoyed the conversation. Mr. Tartiere showed him photos of his son whom he said was the "jeun premier de France," meaning the leading young movie star of France. He also showed photos of his son's wife, the "jeune premier de France." Billy thought he had never seen a more handsome couple.

(He was saddened a few months later at hearing the son had been killed in the early days of World War II. His wife became a heroine of the Resistance.)

So far, the war in Europe had only touched Billy's generation very lightly. He had driven up to Middleburg to open his office the same day Hitler had invaded Poland.

He was greatly excited by the news broadcasts and realized the possibility that he and his friends could be drawn into it, but all this still seemed very far away.

Also, on the radio, he heard Roosevelt say, "I've seen war; I hate war. If I'm elected in November, not one mother's son will die on a foreign battlefield."

By participating in these "extracurricular" activities, Billy was enhancing the prospects of the tavern. Simply having Lucy Lynn and Betty Hubbard there would establish it as the socially correct inn of the hunt country. If run properly, and if it had a really good chef, its fortune would be made.

Billy also realized that he was making a considerable reputation for himself.

It happened that the rear wing of the tavern had a very old tin roof, which needed to be replaced. Under the roof were boards of old pine. There were many kinds of pine growing in the country, but the kind from which this old pine came was one of the finest—a tall tree with medium-long needles, which had grown in abundance in Virginia. It had originally grown in dense forests where it had to grow straight and tall to reach the light. There weren't many large branches except near the top, and so there were only a minimum of knots. The graining and color of the wood were beautiful, particularly where it had been under a roof surface, being baked year after year.

When the obsolete tin was removed from the rear wing, so was the old pine sheathing, and it was used for the millwork of the building. It was beautiful in the cabinets, the benches, the bar in the tap room, and everywhere that fine, natural finish woodwork was important.

When the Tavern was nearly finished, it became obvious that it would need a sign. Billy "sold" the tavern's owners on imitating the signs in Williamsburg, particularly that at the Raleigh Tavern, which he liked very much. Billy designed it himself: a large piece of outdoor plywood, about six-feet high, with eighteenth-century moldings around it, a large simple timber with shaped ends as a support, and ironwork from a local blacksmith to hold it up. The end of the timber was embedded in the stone wall of the building, and projected at an angle so the sign could be viewed from two different roadways.

Mr. Stephenson, at some past time, had found a print of a painting of a fox's head by a renowed eighteenth-century English artists. It only showed the head, which was looking straight at the viewer. It was one of his very favorite things, and he was anxious to have it shown on the sign. The picture had great charm and was right in the character of the building.

Billy was anxious to paint the sign himself. Mr. Stephenson said, "Go ahead and try."

At Mr. Stephenson's three-car garage, one of the spaces was unoccupied. He secured two construction horses, had the mill deliver the sign board there, had it laid out flat on the horses, and had an old table beside it for Billy's paints.

The fox's head was to go in a large oval, about half the height of the sign. Eighteenth-century faux architectural shapes, decorated the sign both above and below the title: Red Fox Tavern, and C. 1728 (circa 1728), the date it was thought the building had originally been started. There were also faux curtains on both sides of the oval, appearing to be behind the architectural shapes. The whole effect met with Billy's approval. He had seen many things like it in Europe.

The most difficult part was the fox's head, which had to be reproduced on a much larger scale. Not only did the fox have to be meticulously executed, and it had to be done twice: the sign had two sides.

Billy enjoyed this type of painting. He was glad that he had indulged his art hobby a great deal before coming to Middleburg. The sign turned out beautifully and was greatly admired. However, it befell that Jack Vietor drove out the next Sunday afternoon to view the almost finished job and the sign. He was very pleased, but he had an inspiration: since the Red Fox Tavern was in the hunt country, and the hunting was preferably for red foxes, the curtain in the sign should be red, not blue. Billy was flabbergasted since he had worked hard to make the very soft, grayed-down blue curtains set off the brighter red fox head.

He was getting one more taste of the life of a "society architect."

The area behind the tavern was turned into a garden. A flagstone terrace was created and surrounded by white dogwood. A large parking area was adjacent. Finally, the project was deemed complete and invitations were sent for a great opening party.

Attractive and prominent people from the worlds of diplomacy, society, and fox hunting flocked to the Tavern. Billy received many compliments.

In Hunt Country, sports, parties, and high living in general seemed paramount. However, there were also a considerable number of prominent and successful people who had settled there, some of whom were of a more serious mold. Paul Mellon had bought a rather large tract of the most beautiful land and was building a handsome house, designed by one of the foremost New York architects, Delano and Aldrich. Mr. Mellon's family connection had distinguished representation in banking, racing, and the top echelons of government. They had given the nation one of its finest art galleries.

The present generation of Mellons was mainly represented by Paul and his cousin Richard. Paul was settling down to the life of a country gentleman, fox hunter, philanthropist, and art collector. Richard Mellon, who lived in Pittsburgh, Pennsylvania, had continued the family's banking tradition. He was also prominent, not only in general business, but also in a successful movement to change the town from a less-than-attractive steel mill town to an attractive, clean, well planned, well run, and cultured place. He, like his cousin Paul, was an enthusiastic fox hunter and was the moving spirit in an outstanding club, the Rolling Rock Club, dear to the hearts of fox hunters, fisherman, party goers, and sportsman in general.

Shortly after the party, the tavern opened for business. One evening, as Billy came in for dinner, Mr. Stevenson appeared and said there was someone there he wanted him to meet. There, alone in the tap room, sat Richard Mellon and his attractive wife, Connie. They said flattering things about the tavern and invited Billy to join them.

Once again, Billy's extracurricular activities came in handy. They spoke of many things, including how Richard was gratifying a lifelong ambition by learning to fly. So was Connie. The evening was a great success. Billy liked the Mellons very much and really thought they liked him. He, of course, could not help being immeasurably excited at this wonderful new contact.

Some time later, after Pearl Harbor, Billy got an important letter from Mr. Mellon asking him to come to Pittsburgh and remodel a house for a friend of his. Billy had already left Middleburg and started work in OP 16 F20 in the Navy Department, and so he had to write Mr. Mellon to decline the invitation. (In his whole life, he had not written a more difficult letter.)

Mr. Stevenson did another fine favor for Billy. Phil and Connie Connors had bought land and intended building a handsome house. He invited them to his house for drinks and to meet Billy, whom he recommended to them highly.

The Connors' land could be reached by an attractive unpaved country road. It sloped gently for 600 yards down to a large stream called Goose Creek in which Mr. Connors loved to fish. There were great competitions with his neighbor to the west regarding the size of the fish caught. This was a constant subject of conversation, which pleased Billy, who also loved fishing.

Billy had little doubt as to which style he should propose for the Connors' house. He had stuck to American eighteenth-century style in the Red Fox Tavern, and had had great success. Middleburg and the country around it was loaded with history. All of the really attractive buildings were from the eighteenth or early nineteenth centuries. They seemed to complement the beautiful countryside, added to which the restoration of Williamsburg had been sensationally well received and had called the entire country's attention to the charm of the old styles. Billy would make it look as much as he possibly could like Carter's Grove, the Wythe House, or Gunston Hall, three grand Williamsburg houses.

Billy, self-confident after his initial success, was sure he could do a top job for the Connors. However, it wasn't that easy. There was an excellent architect in Washington named George Howe. He was attractive, well off, and, by marriage, well connected to the top of society there. Further, and worse, he had a long history of successful practice. Just as Billy was getting well started on the plans, George heard of the project and zeroed in to take it over. He was tough competition.

Billy plunged ahead with the drawings. They seemed to be coming along well. There was a nice view down toward Goose Creek. Billy arranged the living and dining rooms along that side, each with a large bay window. The kitchen and pantry (pantries were still in vogue then) were along the front connecting to the front entrance hall, which also had a winding stair to the second floor. On the opposite side was a large coat closet and powder room, a very small winding masonry stair to the basement and a den.

Mr. Connors wanted what he called a corking room and a wine cellar in the basement, a dark room for photography, and a large basement playroom. There were wings on both ends: on the service end a three-car garage and a utility room; on the other end an office for Mr. Connors opening to the outside for business callers and a large glazed porch to take advantage of the great view on that side. Beneath the glazed porch was the basement playroom.

A major problem appeared. Billy's design was carefully done so as to have a symmetrical center block of the house. All of the really good old homes in the state were that way. Both the style and Billy's design demanded it. Billy was producing a good-looking house. Then Mrs. Connors, who knew nothing about architecture, said she simply hated the idea that because something was done some way on one side, it had to be exactly the same on the other. There went Billy's design.

At the same time, George Howe was practically breathing down Billy's neck; he was so anxious to get the job himself.

Then came unexpected assistance for Billy. At his next conference, Mr. Connors, who was much impressed by social prominence, said, "This morning Lucy Linn rode up to me in the hunting field and said, "'I would like to recommend Mr. Dew to you as your architect.'"

That was potent medicine. That evening Mr. Connors called Billy at home, and said, "George Howe called me saying he had arranged to get a second-hand elevator for us, which would save us a bundle." Billy did his best, and told the truth. "This sounds to me like a clever sales pitch. I think one of the things you don't need is a second-hand elevator. If you've ever been stuck in one you'd know what I mean. I wouldn't have recommended one to you."

Mr. Connors said, "Well, we'll call you back a little later."

The call came. Billy braced himself.

"Are you sitting down? Well, hold on to something." Then there was a pause. "You get the job."

CHAPTER 11

More storm clouds were gathering over Europe and the world.

The war had been simmering all winter. On the Eastern front, things had been going from bad to worse, but nothing yet which appeared really life-threatening to the west. The radio and newspapers were providing plenty for the amateur strategists to worry about, but in general, life went on as "business as usual."

No more.

Late one afternoon, Billy and Mr. Stevenson were at an attractive, old stone house trying to buy box bushes for the tavern. It was getting late and they were invited in for drinks. At six o'clock, someone turned on Lowell Thomas' news hour. The news was like a bomb on the smug, over-confident, semi-isolationist nation. "We now have details of that great battle in the Belgian Forest about which no news had been allowed out. The Nazis have scored a tremendous victory. They have virtually annihilated all resistance in the area. The Panzer Divisions are streaming out in Belgium and toward France. They have gotten almost to Abbeville. Much of the British army has been pushed back into Dunkirk."

Mr. Stevenson remembered enough about France to

point out that if they reached Abbeville, they would have the British cut off.

Day after day, the newspapers and radio carried news of nothing but disaster for the West—the bombing of Amsterdam, the Panzer Divisions rolling virtually unobstructed through France, the thousands fleeing in any way they could, the civilian hordes trying to escape, gasoline supplies running out and bombs dropping.

Billy continued to put all of his time and energy into the Connor's job and believed he was doing it very well. It had now become larger; Mr. Connors had also asked him to design his stable. There was an extra sense of urgency in that most people thought the U.S.A. could probably stay out of the war, but no one was sure.

Neither Mr. nor Mrs. Connors knew anything about architecture, but they were nice employers. Mr. Connors had recently learned to fly and had many stories to tell about it. In those days, few people were pilots; it was regarded as very dangerous. Billy previously had several lessons, and now, with the excitement of the growing war, redoubled his efforts to learn to fly.

From early childhood, he had been fascinated with airplanes and aeronautics. During World War I, before one person in a hundred had even seen a plane, it had happened that the *Lynchburg News* one day was ablaze with headlines saying an airplane was coming to Lynchburg; Lieutenants Menifee and App, then in training at an Army air field, had received permission to fly there and land on the Y.M.C.A. playing field. Billy was agog with excitement and spent the entire afternoon at the field, while his father played golf.

Finally, the crowd burst into a frenzy as someone spotted the distant plane. Billy saw this small object in the sky and it absolutely thrilled him. It circled and landed. Billy, along with the excited crowd, walked all around it, touched it, and examined it. He even wrote the company and got its specifications. It was Curtiss N.J. 4 D-2 "Jenny" training biplane, with small wooden spars between the wings and even between the ailerons. It had numerous wire braces, small rubber tired wheels, bent steel loops beneath each wing tip in case someone got a wing down, separate cockpits, and a wooden tailslide beneath the tail.

From that time on, Billy followed every step in the development of aircraft.

Adolf Hitler not only subjugated much of Europe, and threatened England, but he now cast a long shadow across America. Jack Vietor, who had the dubious privilege of operating the Red Fox Tavern for its first three years (in return for financing the remodeling), volunteered for the Air Force and was now in flight training. He leased the tavern to a Mrs. Gassaway, a formerly successful operator of a Miami Beach restaurant.

Billy was doing his best to finish the house and stable quickly. There was a rumor that all civilian construction might be forbidden. Many qualified young men were now applying for commissions in the armed forces in case the country did go to war.

The knockout punch came from the West, not the East. Billy was at a Sunday luncheon at the house of a retired architect, Mr. Whitfield, who, like many other people in the area, had inherited a large fortune. He had designed many libraries and other buildings for his relatives' charities. Billy was enjoying the stories of his experiences, safe in the memory of days gone by.

They didn't last.

When he left, the radio in his car was recounting

"heavy casualties, devastating damage, tragic losses." Billy was puzzled. Then came the terrible clarification: Japan had attacked Pearl Harbor.

President Roosevelt rolled into the halls of Congress in his wheelchair and, in one of the most forceful speeches of his career, called for a declaration of war on Japan. Congress, with one abstention, passed it.

On the radio the next morning it was announced that Germany and Italy declared war on America. Billy immediately applied for a commission in the Navy. He also did what seemed to be "par for the course," namely going to the Navy building, to the various departments, hoping to be asked for by one that needed a man with his qualifications. The Sea-bees did so. However, they needed him right away. He tried desperately to get his physical exam in time, but couldn't. They had already filled their quota when he took, and presumably passed, the exam and filed his final papers.

The Navy had stationed one officer in its building for the purpose of advising applicants similar to Billy. Billy went straight to him. This officer went over his qualifications carefully, and sent him to the "Identification and Characteristics" section of Navy intelligence. They were impressed with his combination of knowledge of aircraft and his ability to draw, and told him to report for duty as a civilian in Section F-20 until his commission came through. He would work in Washington at first, and then probably be sent to combat zones with air combat intelligence.

The Navy then had very little literature regarding recognition of foreign warships, and virtually none for aircraft. The object of F-20 was, at first, to make large line drawings of these warships from which models and artist's paintings could be made. Intelligence usually had measurements and other data, including good photos of the ships.

The Connors' job was almost finished, and Billy was given enough time to complete the drawings to start construction. The dreaded ruling abolishing all private construction not necessary for the war effort had now been passed, and chances seemed remote that it could be built.

Billy had indicated some fine interior woodwork in the living room, such as cornices and overdoors, very similar to those in Carter's Grove. He had not been able to do full-size details of this. These would be necessary for a good job, but would have required his best talent and skill to have made them really well. It would also have required time. Billy simply had to leave them unfinished.

F-20 was mainly a new thing in the Navy. The section had existed previously, but, like many offices in the prewar Navy, it had been a very weak organization.

Just after Pearl Harbor, a New York architect, Ed Matthews, who had been interested in ships and yachting, had been commissioned to start the graphic work there. Lieutenant Matthews, a bright Princeton graduate now in his late thirties, seemed a perfect choice for the job. He had a charming personality and was very good at dealing with people. He was also well connected in New York.

After a few minor assignments, Billy's first major project was "processing" (making broadside drawings from photographs) the German cruiser Sharnhorst. The waterline length was available from intelligence sources. There were two excellent photos, each from a slight angle and apparently almost identical. Billy selected one of the photos and started his drawing by the method in use in the section, namely, scaling accurately the parts of the ship and repeating them at the required scale on his drawing. Each dimension had to be proportionally altered to the new scale.

Billy had a fine-looking drawing when he gave it to Lieutenant Matthews to be checked. Matthews spent a short time with it and called Billy. He said he had found a number of inaccuracies. Billy was much disturbed, and checked it again himself. The Lieutenant was right—nothing on the drawing was completely right.

Billy could hardly believe this since the drawing was done with great care. When he came in again the next morning, the first thing he did was check the drawing again. Everything on it checked to be perfectly accurate. Billy was astonished. However, he then checked it by the other photo. It checked out to be inaccurate. He had not changed the drawing in any way. He realized the difference had to be between the two pictures.

Still without changing the drawing, he again took it to Lt. Matthews, this time with the photo that checked out to be accurate. Lt. Matthews took a few minutes to inspect the drawing and photo and said, "Yes this is exactly right now."

Billy said, "I've found out something very interesting: our method of processing these ships isn't accurate." He then showed him this other photo and asked him to check it again. With that photo, it checked to be inaccurate.

There was no doubt that the two photos were of the same ship. Billy had now figured out the cause of the trouble. These photos were from a slight angle. The angle in the two was not the same. The dimensions required had to be those along the center line of the ship, which was at something of an angle to the line of sight from the camera, and therefore somewhat foreshortened. Billy, who had led his prep school in trigonometry and had starred in solid geometry, realized that the desired dimension was (in plain view) the hypotenuse of the triangle of which the apparent dimension was the base. It was obvious that the apparently accurate drawing was simply the one which matched the photo Billy had used and that neither matched the real dimensions of the ship.

Billy explained this to Lt. Matthews, but was doubtful that he really understood it. He didn't seem to want to bother with this detail. Nevertheless, before the Lieutenant went off to yet another appointment, Billy got permission to try to develop an accurate method for processing the pictures.

This was far from easy. As far as could be determined, this had never been done before. Virtually all photographs were in some kind of perspective. Billy soon developed proofs that architectural perspective was not really accurate. By looking at photo after photo, however, he finally realized that frequently one could see enough parallel lines to get vanishing points.

With these vanishing points, he finally produced a system, which proved much more accurate than the old way.

Lt. Matthews, not having a technically-oriented mind, either forgot about this matter in the excitement of the time, or did not consider it very important. Section F-20's mission was primarily to produce graphic products for recognition purposes, which did not demand extreme accuracy.

Billy had already received a severe shock. His application for commission had been denied. He had not passed the physical exam. There were too many spots on his lung from the tuberculosis attack he had in college and the pneumonia he had suffered previously.

Also, the F.B.I. had made an error. In the original application, the form had called for his first name, middle initial, and last name. Billy had written "William B. Dew, Jr." He had a first cousin whose name was William Braxton Dew, who had a brilliant mind, but a bad alcohol problem and had once, while drinking, gotten in a fight with a cop. Billy thought of this, and went back to one of his superior officers. He explained that he believed his and his cousin's records had been confused. The F.B.I. made another check and agreed. Billy took this back to Commander Hibberd, a fine naval officer, who told him he would now get his commission.

However, time wore on, and the commission didn't come through. It may have been that Matthews, who hadn't even really understood Billy's "perspective method," was blocking it. Matthews was having fine success as it was; no one was making final checks of his products. They were used only for making models, large paintings, and recognition studies. Everyone was happy.

There were several other young men already in the new section who, like Billy, were expecting commissions. One morning there was a new one, Ensign Lavoy. He was the first one at work and applied himself very seriously to his task. Lt. Matthews put him in charge of submarine matters and drawings. Matthews had received a good recommendation for him from a prominent modern architect, Saarinen, for whom he had worked. Matthews said Lavoy was so good that he should have other people around just to pick up things and run errands. This struck a raw nerve in Billy, who had grown up in the shadow of Polly Cary, and had been accustomed to being overlooked and snubbed in almost everything in his early days at Sweet Briar.

Soon Matthews, who was enjoying his contacts around

the navy building, was having ideas about virtually letting Lavoy run the section. Lavoy soon developed similar ideas.

Matthews had either completely forgotten Billy's system or didn't care to fuss with it. It really wasn't easy to understand. The section, staffed with embryo architects, was turning out beautiful drawings. Actually, most of them were accurate enough for the purpose.

The section, and another whose responsibility was statistics, were both under the authority of a higher officer, Commander Moore, who was an Annapolis graduate. He was a "retread," having previously retired and come back after Pearl Harbor. Billy thought he would probably have been a good seagoing officer, but there was no reason he should have known anything (and he didn't) about architectural drawing. He liked the good-looking drawings F-20 was turning out. No one checked them for complete accuracy.

Lt. Matthews, a yachtsman himself, considered merchant ships less than socially acceptable. Also, when someone asked him whether he liked airplanes, he said, "No, they make too much noise." He was soon unhappy when an enormous order came into the section to produce broadside diagrams of every ship in the Japanese merchant marine. This required not only working with loathsome merchant ships, but it also required extreme accuracy. This wasn't his style. It was not only for identification, but also for the subs, at least in certain circumstances, the drawings had to be accurate enough by which to aim. A less than completely accurate drawing could mean a miss. Lt. Matthews never showed the slightest interest in the project.

The ship diagrams were finished by the promised date. Hal Lindley had already determined the format: a classification of the entire Japanese merchant marine by certain easily recognized characteristics by which an observer could, without turning a page, run down from large groups to smaller groups, to the exact model. In many cases, there were numerous identical sister ships, so that only identifying the model would be enough. These charts and ship diagrams were bound into neat booklets and circulated to the fleet.

Sometime later on, the Commander-in-Chief's office sent a memo saying this work was completely satisfactory and directing the section to make a similar one of every merchant marine ship in the world.

When this happened, Billy had already left the merchant ship section. Shortly before finishing the ship assignment, he was appointed aircraft analyst. He had been extremely interested in the merchant ship project, but aircraft analyst was what he had really always wanted.

Somewhat earlier, Lavoy, whose ambition was, amongst other things, to control all of the publishing for the section, had attempted to make a small booklet for identification of American aircraft, probably wanting to follow it with similar pamphlets on foreign ones. This attempt was a colossal failure. Amongst other things, he made four ridiculous errors. For instance, he called the Grumman Wildcat F-4-F the F-47. Also, for the consolidated Catalina PBY (a twin-engine plane), he showed two pictures, one a correct one and the other a four-engine flying boat, the Consolidated Coronado. There were two other equally glaring errors.

Japan, very weak in natural resources, having no oil, no rubber, little steel, and lacking various necessary chemicals, was totally dependent on its merchant marine. Anything that would help our submarines in sinking them was of top importance.

There was in F-20 already an excellent merchant ship

analyst, Hal Lindley. He had not been to an Ivy League college and so was completely out of the social side of the section. However, he had years of experience at sea and knew ships and everything about them.

Billy, not impressed with the social side of the war, was thrilled when the job was dumped into his lap. He never knew whether Matthews had belatedly recognized the importance of his perspective method, or whether Matthews had disliked him after the two ship pictures incident. He suspected the latter, since he had cast doubts on the accuracy of Matthews' way of processing ship pictures.

The merchant ship analyst, Hal Lindley, was very helpful and easy going. He sometimes seemed the only one in the section that really knew what he was doing. Billy had one assistant, a very bright young high school graduate, Paul Buchanan, whom he had brought into the section himself.

That summer was terribly hot. This little merchant ship group was working in the top floor of the building. There was a flat roof over them and another immediately outside at the level below of the very large windows that let in excellent light for working. It also let in the radiant heat of the roof on several days when the thermometer reached slightly over 100 degrees. There was yet no air conditioning in the building. However, there was one advantage of this location. It was free from Lavoy, who had been making himself a nuisance downstairs.

There was then very little in the aircraft files in O.N.I. Also, there was tremendous pressure to get an aircraft recognition book out to the training facilities and the fleet. Billy immediately started working hard to build up the picture file sufficiently to do this. There was no one source in the building for them. Billy had to go to office after office to find them.

Meanwhile, Lavoy, whose ambition was to have credit for all publishing in F-20, was making himself a nuisance, taking up Billy's time trying to force him to turn over his pictures to him. Realizing that Lavoy knew nothing about aircraft, and remembering the ridiculously poor attempt he had made before, Billy, as diplomatically as possible, ignored him.

Billy, in addition to his search for adequate pictures, also read the secret intelligence reports, which were extremely interesting, but took a certain amount of time.

It happened at this time that the mainland U.S.A. on the Pacific coast was bombed. This did no damage except start a small forest fire, which went out of its own accord. It got virtually no notice in the press, but was considered fairly important by military intelligence.

It was obviously done somehow by aircraft. Even before Midway there had been no Japanese carriers anywhere within range of California. The admirals were puzzled.

As aircraft analyst, Billy was consulted. He not only said an air attack was possible, but identified the airplane: a very small float plane, which the Japanese had designed for this purpose. It could be broken down sufficiently to get into one of their subs, then very easily and quickly be assembled at night on the sub's deck and in calm weather, take off and land on the water.

Its intended target was unknown. The pilot at night apparently didn't navigate very well and wasted his small bomb load on open country.

Lt. Matthews seemed more preoccupied with his contacts around the navy building and left more in the section to Lavoy.

Billy was fast building up the airplane photo files, but there was still virtually nothing of Russian aircraft. One morning, he received a written order to go to New York for two days and report to O.N.I.'s very secret office there.

They, in turn, sent him to an agent in the office of a popular New York newspaper. There, he was given a false name and pressman's union card. This agent made an appointment for him at Pravda's office with the cover story that he was writing something for their Sunday paper on the great things the Russians were doing with aircraft design and manufacture. To make his article valid, he told the Russians he wanted to get whatever photos he could of their planes.

Billy found this very exciting and did get some pictures.

On returning to the navy building, Billy found that Lavoy had engineered having his office and all his files moved from the main building to a temporary one beside his own. This was a considerable handicap since Billy had to walk to and over a bridge to the main building where most of the sources of the pictures were. Billy suspected that Lavoy had also promoted his New York trip in order to get this done when he couldn't object. It was now perfectly clear that Lavoy was trying to get complete authority over the aircraft operation, never mind that Billy's picture collecting would be considerably handicapped. Commander Moore, being incompetent to handle the architects, and being encouraged by Lt. Matthews to do so, was now leaning heavily toward depending on Lavoy to run the section.

Billy still frequently saw Hall Lindley, who told him that he had been warned that a commissioned officer might be put in his section. By Navy rules, this officer would have final authority there. There was little doubt that Lavoy was promoting this and would put someone he controlled himself there for the purpose of getting control of the section. Lavoy was still Lt. Matthews' pet, and Commander Moore was unlikely to oppose him. Lindley, a civilian, told Billy he would resign if this happened. Billy knew that Matthews would like to have an all Ivy League section there, and suspected that he and Lavoy weren't really pleased at the great success of the Japanese merchant ship book.

A few weeks previously, a very fine commercial artist, Rolf Klep, had joined the section and had already produced a good monotone painting of a battleship. He called on Billy. "I understand you are getting together really good material for an aircraft recognition handbook. My job is to get these things ready for publication. Let me know as soon as you are ready. We should work together on the format and any special things in it."

Rolf Klep was older, experienced, and unlike the sometimes childish and always grasping Lavoy, a reasonable man. Billy was a little disappointed since he had given great thought to the format of the book, but it was clear that he should cooperate with Rolf. He thought Rolf would go along with his ideas.

Aircraft identification had previously been handled by a different part of O.N.I. Once again, there was nobody there who had a material interest in it or knew much about it. They had pushed a system called W.E.F.T. (wings, engine, tail, fuselage). The student was supposed to learn the type of wings, how many engines, what type of fuselage, (i.e., how many gun turrets, the general shape), and the type tail (one or two rudders, etc.). When someone saw an airplane, he was supposed to mentally add all these things up and remember what type of plane matched them. This was cumbersome and unsatisfactory. Billy had been an expert on the identification of planes for years and realized that to know a certain model airplane by sight covers all of these things and is fully and instantly usable in combat.

He was now ready to start the identification manual. It was first to be divided into different booklets, one for the aircraft of each country. Commander Moore wouldn't permit this. He wanted one for the whole world initially. This knocked out making a start almost immediately and getting it out to the fleet.

Billy thought the idea of putting an officer in Lindley's section simply revolting. It was the only thing in F-20 that had been consistently running well.

He soon found that he himself was about to receive a similar blow. One morning, Commander Moore came in and put a note on his desk. "Tomorrow morning, Ensign Richard Myrick will join you to assist in your work."

He duly appeared at 8 o'clock, in his new uniform. Billy thought he had never met a nicer young man, but there was one problem with him personally: he knew absolutely nothing about aircraft. Now Billy, in addition to his own load of work, had to find things that Myrick was reasonably able to do to keep him busy.

This problem solved itself. Every time Billy left the office, Myrick removed from the files more of his pictures and turned them over to Lavoy. (Billy soon found out that Myrick had been a friend of Lavoy for years.) The situation became still more complicated. While Billy was forbidden to start publishing the much needed identification manual, Lavoy was already trying to concoct a bootleg one. He even brought it in for Billy to check for him. Billy did examine it. It was little better than his previous effort—full of errors and no particular clarity in the format.

Commander Moore himself was descended on by a superior, a four-stripe captain who was examining the section. In the process, he told the Commander they needed action on the aircraft manual. Commander Moore, obviously in trouble, tried for an excuse. "Until we had Myrick here, we didn't have anyone who knew anything about aircraft."

Billy could barely refrain from giving the Captain an earful. (Possibly he should have done so.)

For the next few days, Billy became more discouraged. He remembered the Japanese merchant ship book and how with no one bothering them they had worked hard, wasted no time, and produced a satisfactory manual in reasonable time. Perhaps he had been wrong in not throwing his weight behind Lavoy. He didn't think that would have been nearly as good a solution. If he could simply have worked with Rolf Klep, possibly have had one or two assistants, and had the backing of Lt. Matthews, and had no interference from Lavoy, he could have done for aircraft what he and Lindley had done for merchant ships. Aircraft identification had been bandied about and neglected in the Navy and never had been under anyone who was really deeply interested in it. Under the present officers in F-20, an overage retiree who knew very little about the kind of things Billy was doing and had no grasp of events there, and a New York socialite, Lt. Matthews, all Billy could see in the future was more of the same. As a civilian, he didn't have enough rank to do much about it.

Billy composed a letter resigning his civilian employment in the Navy. He considered it for several days before presenting it. Amongst other things, he hoped it would bring Commander Moore and possibly the appropriate higher officer to their senses regarding aircraft matters.

He realized he could be criticized for walking out on them when the going got rough. If this were true, however, all they had to do to make him stay was ask.

He did present the letter. They did not ask him to reconsider. There was no one left in the section that knew much about or had any special interest in aircraft.

Billy tried for a commission in the Marines, but was turned down for medical reasons. He soon heard that Lindley didn't resign; he was fired. (After the war, he learned that Hal Lindley had become port director of a principle port in India, and, later, director of all ports in India.) He also heard that Lavoy's vaulting ambition had landed him in trouble: the Navy only temporarily swallowed his publishing dreams.

Billy immediately informed his draft board that he was no longer with the Navy. He soon got an induction notice, but once again failed the physical. He then gave up his attempts at the armed services and got a job in an aircraft plant making engines for B-29's. He was in charge of designing any special carriers needed to transport engine parts in the plants. This was interesting to him, and took him all over each of the seven plants in the area. It was not long before he could identify virtually any part in the engine and knew how to deal with it. Some of the microfinished parts had a tolerance of $\pm$ 1,000,000th of an inch. Some were silver plated and were beautiful things to behold.

One day, Billy was down in plant number seven, and he happened to go to a certain department to which some of the personnel who had been with him in plant number two had gone. Someone told him that his office was trying hard to contact him to tell him to call his sister in Ridgewood.

Polly Cary said his father, whose heart trouble had been worsening for some time, was very ill, and Billy and she should go home immediately. Bill Woodson, who had often been at Sweet Briar, had called the railroad representative in New York in connection with getting the girls home and back on vacations, and had made arrangements for Polly Cary and Billy to ride the prime train, which soon left New York. From the train, Billy called "Dr. Will" Walker, and asked him to meet them in Monroe and bring them home.

William was in the Baptist Hospital, the best one in Lynchburg. Natalie had seen to it that he had the best corner room in the building. He had said, "The main trouble with people dying is that everyone has to come so far to be with them."

William lasted several days. Finally, the family was told one evening that that night would probably be his last. It was agreed that only Billy would go over to the hospital. Natalie was not strong enough, and Polly Cary would stay with her mother.

When Billy got back to the hospital, he was told that he might visit his father for a few minutes, and whatever happened, he was not to stay long. Just as Billy was leaving, his father thought of something else he would like to say. Billy stopped to hear it, and then again, just as he was leaving, William thought of something else to say. Billy continued to leave. For the rest of his life, he regretted not having heard the last thing his father wanted to tell him, as William passed away shortly after Billy left the room.

CHAPTER 12

As the allied armies rolled closer to Berlin and the Army, Navy, and Marines, although with terrible casualties, came closer to Tokyo, the production of B-29's began to be cut rather than increased. Men were being laid off faster in Billy's factory. Billy found out that the large firm of York and Sawyer in New York had the contract to design the Army's new hospital in the Hawaiian Islands. They were trying hard to build up their team of architects. He immediately contacted Mr. Kiff at their organization, who assured him a job at a vastly higher salary than he was now receiving.

So Billy started work in New York; however, he knew nothing about hospital architecture. Mr. Kiff soon transferred him to a project designing new buildings at Rutgers University. This went much better, but it still lacked the freedom he felt in Middleburg. A prominent New York architect, Mr. William Creighton, was in charge of the section. Mr. Creighton had had a most successful practice in New York before the war. It happened that Jock Whitney had selected him to remodel Langollan Farm, near Middleburg. He had also designed the famous horseshoe-shaped barn there.

But Billy was still not happy. He had had the thrill of

running his own business in Middleburg very successfully. Having someone over him just wasn't his dish. He applied to one of the best architects in New York and was accepted.

His first job was to work on the Our Lady of Victory Church way down near Wall Street. This was going very well when something he hadn't anticipated occurred: Hitler's final jab, the Battle of the Bulge. The Catholic Church was counting on government money to complete the project, and funds were now cut off. They kept him several weeks and then let him go.

One of the best things that had ever happened to Billy was just before the previous summer when he had stopped by 51 Fifth Avenue looking for an apartment. They had none, but said there was a Mr. Bond living there who might let him sublet for the summer. Mr. Bond was the private secretary to the editor of *The New York Times*. His apartment was not very large, but was crammed with van Loon watercolors. Mr. Bond was a great friend of Hendrick van Loon. He invited Billy to dinner and everything was arranged.

Billy gave himself a long, beautiful vacation in New York City, where he loved the museums, the theater, and the opera. He then loaded all of his belongings into his little Plymouth convertible and set out for Middleburg.

In Middleburg, there was the ubiquitous housing shortage of the times. There were no attractive apartments for rent. The Red Fox Tavern was far too expensive. Billy spent a day looking, then settled for a large comfortable room in the Luck House, where most of the fox hunting group had stayed at one time or another.

This proved interesting. In one room, there was the young minister of one of the town's churches. Billy didn't consider him interesting, but across the hall there was a small apartment inhabited by an attractive young lady. She spent much of her time in her room, apparently working on something. Soon it happened that once she left her door open. Billy saw inside an easel and several large canvasses.

There was a telephone in the hall. The young lady was just hanging up once when Billy came through. She said, "Hello."

Billy said, very politely, "I believe you're an artist."

"Yes, I am."

"Could I see some of your work some time? I'm an architect."

"Come in right now. I'll show you some of it. I'm Jean Penticost."

"This looks great. Do you always paint horses?" Billy asked.

"Yes, I love fox hunting, and they're about all I do," she replied.

"Why are there so many horses heads? They almost seem to be portraits, except of horses. Do you ever paint people?" Billy was delighted by her work.

"No, I hate to paint people. These are heads of favorite hunters of some of my friends over in Clark County. They are nice things for them to keep," Gene said.

"You seem to paint very well. I would think you might find a fine market for portraits of their children. Do you ever do things like that?"

"No, I hate children."

Later that afternoon, there came a knock on Billy's door. It was Jean. "I would like to ask a favor. Alex Mackay Smith, from over in Clark County, is coming over this evening. Could you possibly let him in and entertain him until I get ready to go out with him? I'm afraid Mrs. Luck would be shocked if he came up to my room."

Billy agreed.

Alex Mackay Smith, tall, good looking, very urbane, and an interesting raconteur, arrived at nearly the appointed time. After the usual courtesies, Alex said, "You have an unusual name. Do you have an ancestor who was president of William and Mary University before the Civil War?"

"Yes, how on earth did you know that?" Billy asked.

"I live in the house where he was married. He was one of the main political writers and philosophers of the era. He married the niece of George Burwell, who owned Carter Hall," said Alex.

It happened shortly after this that Billy received a phone call from the Reverend Mr. Riley, the Episcopal minister in Upperville, a neighboring village, who had impressed Billy by holding service with World War I bravery medals on his vestments. "I have found out about a contract you might be able to get. Wing Commander Tony Wilson of the Royal Canadian Air Force and his wife have bought an old house near Paris and expect to remodel it drastically. They asked me to call you. You can call them at 3751."

Billy, very excited, found the place, a small house, which was really a connected group of several small, pretty stone buildings. "I think this is most attractive," he told Mrs. Wilson.

"Thank you. I bought it several years ago, and when I got my divorce and moved out of Carter Hall, I connected this nice tiny cottage with the garage and smoke house, cleaned the trash out of them, finished the insides and settled here. I'm tired of living in large houses; I've done it all my life. This little thing, right in the midst of my garden, just hit the nail on the head for me; but now that I've remarried, my husband and I need something much bigger."

"Mr. Wilson is Canadian?"

"I want you to meet him. He's English. He'll be back from the general store in Paris in a few minutes. He was in the R.A.F., but he had a terrible auto wreck, a bad concussion, and was invalided out of the R.A.F. because he could no longer fly at high altitudes. We got married then and came back to this country. When the war started, to do his bit, he went back into the Canadian Air Force as an instructor. Here he comes now."

Tony Wilson was even more impressive than Mackay-Smith: taller, and with the nice smooth accent of the Eton trained British aristocracy. "Thank you for coming. Emily and I have bought something that needs a genius to put it in livable shape. Let's go over and look at it."

The house was on top of high ground in one of the prettiest parts of horse country. It had a great view but wasn't much of a house itself. Tony Wilson was entertaining, and he and Billy had a nice chat about flying. Billy was to make a sketch and call them again. The sketch was simple, and Billy thought the design could be within the budget they had given him, which was rather low. They suggested and Billy made some revisions and then called them again.

Tony said, "My brother Peter has come out for the weekend and brought a friend, Tom Waterman, who has been writing excellent books on old American houses. They got very excited about the house, and Tom is going to make some drawings. He did excellent work at Williamsburg and is really quite well known. Peter is on leave from his auction house in London. He is considered to be an expert on old houses."

Billy was duly upset, particularly when he saw Tom's sketches, which were beautiful, but which indicated a house some $100,000 more expensive than the limit they had given him. Billy's disappointment was particularly bitter because he had gotten along with the Wilsons so well and thought they would be ideal clients and perhaps friends.

By chance, he encountered the Reverend Riley on the street and recounted what had happened. "Don't feel too bad. Tom Waterman is the toughest of competition. He was the ace designer at Williamsburg, and he has just published the best of books on seventeenth and eighteenth century buildings in America. He is the apartment mate of Tony's brother Peter, who is also no pushover. He seems slated to be head of his auction house, Southeby's, which is the second largest in London. He is one of the top experts on English antiques." He continued, "Tony's family is interesting. His grandfather, Lord Ribbelsdale, has been called one of the most powerful men in Edwardian England. There is a beautiful Sergeant portrait of him, a very tall man leaning against a column, and also a group portrait of three of his cousins, the Windham sisters. His father, called Scathers, by the way, much less serious minded, has been called the leading playboy of England."

A few days later, Billy felt somewhat better about this matter when Emily Wilson invited him to a party. She apologized profusely and nicely for having disappointed him. (Billy suspected that Mr. Riley had put her up to it.)

Billy was unable to retain any ill feelings toward the Wilsons. Tony said he was going to make an airstrip on his farm and buy an airplane. He asked Billy to help him select one and said they all would all enjoy it.

CHAPTER 13

Billy discovered that Mr. Conners had indeed been able to build his house, and he was soon invited to a party there. (He also soon realized that, in horse country, a bachelor is frequently a sought-after social item.) Billy was very dissatisfied with the house. The places where it should have been symmetrical were exactly as he had been forced to draw them asymmetrical. Inside, he thought it a real mess. The nice winding stairway he had designed to the second floor was not there. There was a narrow hallway cutting through between the entrance hall and the living room. The cute little winding stone stair to the basement wasn't there. Worst of all, the fine overdoors in the living room, the large details, which he hadn't been able to finish before leaving for the war, were there, but had been detailed by the mill and were out of scale with everything else and unattractive.

A few days before, Billy had gone to dinner at the Red Fox Tavern. He had noticed a nice couple also dining there. He found out that they were a leading doctor from Washington and his son, who were new residents near Middleburg. The son, John Talbot, had slight traces of a hair lip. Nevertheless, the young ladies of the community seemed to consider him handsome. He was also at the

Connors' party, and he and Billy were soon in conversation, which drifted to aeronautics.

John asked, "You like to fly, don't you?"

"Yes, I've been doing it whenever I feel rich enough."

"That's lucky. I bought an airplane today. I got it from army surplus disposal for only a thousand dollars. It's a Fairchild P.T. 19. Why don't you go over to the airport with me someday and we'll check it out?" asked John.

Billy knew the P.T. 19 was the standard Army Air Corps primary trainer. He also knew it was much heavier and faster, and almost three times as powerful as the Piper Cubs he had been flying. He recalled once in Lynchburg he had seen some of the Navy recruits learning to fly in the Navy's equivalent plane, the "Yellow Peril," a biplane trainer. One recruit was trying to land; the plane was starting to "ground loop," and he lost control of it. By wonderful luck, it went exactly sideways at the intersecting runway. He succeeded in gunning it into a take-off along that runway, and an accident was averted. This was a frightening experience for both pilot and spectators.

John Talbot was having his plane painted, but it was finally ready. For Billy, still smarting from his frustration while with the Navy, this chance to fly a service aircraft almost seemed a means of getting even with the military. The nearer to the plane they got though, the scarier this army plane seemed to be. John Talbot was also losing his aplomb. The wings had been taken off for painting. How could they be certain they had been put back on right? By the time they got to the airplane, John was beginning to shake. "I'm too scared; I'm not going to fly it today."

Billy took one look at this sleek, streamlined craft, and also wished he were somewhere else. But he mustered his courage. "I'm going to try it. There'll be an instructor with me, he doesn't want to be killed either."

The head of the little airport was just out of the service. They understood he had been a Marine flying instructor. They also understood he was so mean that the air field was losing business. He was a large, rather harsh-looking man.

In the plane, the instructor proceeded to tell Billy the basics of how to take off. Billy's heart sank. He had expected the instructor to be doing the flying at least on the first flight. Billy taxied to the end of the runway. The instructor told him to stop, made him check the engine temperature, and explained clearly and concisely some things about operating the plane. Billy turned down the runway and gave it full power. Before they were even in the air, he knew he liked the ship. He climbed to 400 feet, made a 90-degree turn, climbed to 600 feet, made another turn, and leveled off. "This doesn't seem so terribly hard after all," thought Billy.

The instructor told him to make a right turn, then several more turns, then told him to make an approach and land.

"My God, he expects me to land this thing!"

Billy by now was having a wonderful time. He lined up with the runway, but was considerably too high. He had now gotten the idea: "Go ahead and fly the damn thing. This instructor isn't going to let me get in any really bad trouble." He gave it a side slip to lose altitude, then gave it another. The instructor said nothing. Billy crossed the end of the runway very low, and started little by little pulling the stick back as he felt the plane slowing. Finally, the wheels touched, and he was simply taxiing up the runway.

The instructor turned around in his seat. "What makes you think you can learn to fly? You haven't done anything right yet. You didn't make a single turn 90 degrees. Even you ought to know not to land with the brakes on. Okay, I can stand it, take it around again."

Billy took off with no trouble, climbed to 400 feet, and made a left 90-degree turn. He then climbed to 600 feet, flew parallel with the runway, made another 90-degree turn, and started descending.

The instructor slapped the stick hard sideways. The plane rolled almost on its side and started into a dive. Billy helped it into a shallow dive and then easily pulled out of it. He turned the plane into a long arc to get lined up with the runway, came on in, and made another good landing. He was now finding that this plane was easier to fly than the Piper Cub.

On the ground, the instructor rose to new heights of vituperation. He screamed about incompetent execution of turns and use of brakes. He even jumped out of his cockpit and stuck his face into Billy's. "I'm not willing to risk my life with you one more minute, take it around by yourself this time." He turned and started to stride away, then stopped, returned, and patted Billy on the back. "Go ahead, kid, you can do it."

Actually, this instructor had Billy in a bold state of mind, which was practically perfect for this solo flight. It went without a hitch.

John Talbot had a nice farm on the banks of a large stream about five miles from Middleburg. Billy had now, perhaps unfortunately, completely lost his fear of the P.T.19. He decided to fly over and buzz John on his farm. He knew some simple maneuvers he had learned in his pre-solo days in the Piper Cub. On a fine day, perfect for flying, he filled the plane with gas, flew over a low mountain range, and easily found the farm. He rolled the plane over on its side as he had seen the Navy dive bombers do in the movies. He steered it straight down into a dive, pulled out of the dive, did several stalls, then performed "lazy eights." (He understood that it took a good flyer to do these things exactly right, but his were plenty good enough to look spectacular from the ground.) Then he took a dive, flew over the farm at low altitude, waving at John as he went by, and headed back over the mountain to the air field. He had a wonderful time, and his new friend was duly impressed.

Billy later called up John. "This is a wonderful plane you have. It flies without using any gas at all. I flew well over an hour, and when I got back the gas gauge still registered full."

"That gauge is okay. The plane has just been n.c.'d; there is nothing wrong with it."

It happened that Billy had already picked up a client—a very attractive one. Kitty Dudley had called and taken him out to see an old house she had just bought about 15 miles from Middleburg. It had obviously been built around the late nineteenth century. The four or five steps up to the porch were flanked with huge yellow terra cotta lions. At the left end, the walls bulged forward at 45 degrees so as to form something like a large bay window, yet they went all the way up to the top of the second story. The front door had a large pane of glass, frosted into a fancy design.

Kitty Dudley was obviously exceptionally good company. "I am expecting my divorce any day now. I may soon be remarried and need this house very quickly," she told Billy.

Billy took complete measurements of the house, made drawings, and proceeded to trace over them with changes he thought should be made. He soon was able to achieve a scheme, which would be simple and beautiful. The changes necessary would be drastic. He had learned something from the Wilson adventure: don't be too modest in the initial design.

There came a beautiful day and Billy planned to go over to the air field and have a nice long flight. He was almost ready to leave when Kitty called. "I want to see those sketches you're making. I'll be there about 3:30." Billy made a weak try to get out of it, without any luck.

Later that evening, John Talbot called. "I'll tell you what happened this afternoon. I went over to the field, and the other instructor took me up for a lesson. We climbed to 400 feet, and the engine stopped. The propeller was absolutely still in the air; we were out of gas. The instructor put it into a glide, then put it into such a slip it seemed we were going almost straight down. We were fortunate to land in a field without hurting anything."

Billy knew it had been flown at least once since his last flight. He felt sure he would have "gassed it up" before flying, since he was suspicious of the gauge. Nevertheless, he thought Kitty Dudley might possibly have saved his life.

CHAPTER 14

It had been noticed that on Saturday evenings in Middleburg, the country people came to town and liked to parade up and down the street, look in the modest store windows, perhaps have a Coca-Cola, and see all their friends. Although they liked to do this, there was a movement to try to improve the town for them, try to give them something better to do.

A meeting took place one evening of various public-spirited citizens to discuss these improvements. There was already a small movie theater. No one seemed to know what should be done, but everyone was in a good humor what with the war being won and people beginning to come home.

Billy attended the meeting. There were a number of suggestions but no consensus. One of the most interested people seemed to be Howell Jackson, an ex-General Motors vice-president, the descendant of a distinguished Southern family, and the owner of one of the very best racing stables in Europe. Billy introduced himself to Mr. Jackson.

"I am an architect. I have studied in Europe, worked for Maurice Fatio in Palm Beach, and I have already remodeled the Red Fox Tavern here. Perhaps I could help with this project. I would be very glad to do anything I could," he said.

Mr. Jackson, a man of great energy and at that time not much to focus it on, was also interested in this "experiment in democracy." He thought it was just the thing to find a talented person in the town to head the project. He invited Billy to dinner to discuss it.

Billy, once again in a great state of excitement, drove his little convertible out past the meadows bordering the town, down into a deep hollow, over a little bridge across Little River, and turned through simple, country stone gate posts into the Jackson's land. Their road was simple sand and clay, the preferred type in the country. He soon came to a long, low dry stone wall on one side, planted with random dogwood trees, bulbs and small shrubs, all of which seemed to go naturally with the wide strip of perfectly mown grass on both sides of the road. At the top of the gradual slope, the road turned toward the house. One could see only the wings and upper parts of most of it over a 15-foot clipped hemlock hedge around the large parking area in front. As one came closer, more of the good-looking house could be seen through a wide opening in the hedge where the road came through.

Inside, the house designed by one of the best New York residential architects was beautifully arranged and detailed. Dorothy Jackson, Howell's new wife, had exquisite taste in architecture and decoration, and, as heiress of the National Cash Register Co. fortune, the means to perform. Every room was a triumph of beautiful pictures, furniture, architectural details, silver, porcelain, rugs, curtains and even small miscellaneous items, which added to the charm.

On entering the house, one could walk past the powder

room and bar to the living room, or one could go straight ahead through the library door across the library and through another door to the outside terrace. There one could see one of the most thoroughly attractive views in the hunt country.

Billy was the only guest. The occasion was very successful. Billy loved quail and dove shooting. One of Mr. Jackson's main current interests was a 1,000-plus-acre shooting preserve in the Bull Run Mountains, small mountains three or four miles away, which stretched for many miles across the view from his rear terrace and greatly beautified it.

Dorothy Jackson loved Florence, Italy, almost as much as Billy did, and they enjoyed reliving their memories of it.

All three talked long into the evening about the community project in Middleburg. The more they discussed what it should be, the more interested the Jacksons became in the project. One of the people who was pushing the project, Charley Cushman, a businessman, had already suggested that what the entire community needed was a really nice place to have parties, meetings, exhibits, and possibly plays. Billy suggested a possible little theater group.

This was before the days of integration, and Howell Jackson was emphatic in his opinion that there should also be a nice facility for the blacks and that at least as much money in proportion to their numbers should be spent on them as on that for the white members of the community.

Billy, remembering a few attractive open air theaters he had seen in gardens in Europe, suggested one here as a comparatively inexpensive way of seating a large audience and as more comfortable on warm evenings than a non-air-conditioned building. He also suggested a swimming pool as one of the best things they could have. If possible, there should be a large playing field for softball, football practice, touch football, and youth baseball. He also suggested a bowling alley. Mr. and Mrs. Jackson were prepared to make material financial contributions to the project. It was also thought that Mr. Paul Mellon would help materially. A further fund-raising campaign was planned.

Before the end of the evening, it was decided that Billy should submit preliminary sketches for a building with a small entrance foyer, a large all-purpose room, a stage, dressing rooms, a service kitchen, perhaps movie projection equipment, an office and perhaps a bowling alley.

Mr. Jackson thought he knew of a suitable small tract of land in the town which could be bought.

Billy hardly waited until the next morning to start sketches of the building. He would retain the essence of what he thought Middleburg should be: a town in which all new buildings should go with the existing eighteenth- and nineteenth-century buildings like the Red Fox Tavern. He would have loved to have created an ambiance similar to Williamsburg, but he realized this was impossible.

Billy's design was similar to what might have been found in Williamsburg, but with proportions more similar to those of the very good old buildings in Middleburg. It included everything as tentatively agreed, except Billy went all out for the stage, with wings, dressing rooms, a green room, and even a scenery making room and large store room. Unfortunately, these extra things produced too large a building, and the backers of the project didn't accept them.

The large lot was purchased and a contour survey made. Billy, working with Mr. Jackson, fitted the building outline into it in such a way that it was back from the street, with a large open plaza, at least 40 feet x 40 feet in front of it, to give importance, to make the facade more visible, and to give space for the audience to collect when shows would be given in nice weather. One side of the large room (40 feet x 60 feet), was to open on a flagstone terrace, which was also to be part of the stage for the outdoor theater.

At the rear of the building was to be a parking space and beyond that, at a higher elevation, a honey locust grove was to be made into a small park. To the side of that, the property stretched away for a considerable distance, and there would be room for the playing field.

Along the front street, the next building was a small house. This was bought to be the manager's house. Between this and the open air theater there was a strip about 20 feet wide, which would become a garden. Mrs. Paul Mellon, an expert on gardens, agreed to develop it.

Behind the open-air theater another strip was to become a small children's play ground. In this, Billy suggested placing a small splashing pool, only 21 inches maximum depth.

Immediately behind the open-air theater would be the main swimming pool with a small snack pavilion and on another side, bath houses.

The town hall project had been booming. Billy had been having almost daily meetings with Dorothy and Howell Jackson. They were working out a beautiful building on lovely, appropriate grounds. Billy was doing what most architects don't usually do: making large-scale, carefully studied interior elevations in addition to those of the exterior. Every door, every cornice, every pilaster had its full-size detail. In the auditorium, a problem was that there were windows over windows. Billy found that, inside, they looked infinitely better if curtained as if opening vertically. This meant details of the curtains and full-size details of the valences had to be carefully done to harmonize with the adjacent pilaster capitals.

The building, like most buildings, had its problems. From the foyer, the stairs went up to the second and third floors, which had a large American Legion room. They also went down to the bowling alley. Also from the foyer, three large double doors led into the auditorium. This, unless remedied, would never pass the state fire marshal's code, and could be considered an undesirable hazard. (A fire in the auditorium, far from an unprecedented event, could quickly spread to the foyer and stairs and trap anyone on the floors above.)

The foyer, including the three double doors, was beautifully detailed in raised panel-type old pine. There were several types of commercial fire doors on the market, any of which would have completely ruined the design and the general atmosphere of the building. Billy, after several sleepless nights, finally concocted a very unusual design: a 2¼ inch thick sandwich door, old pine paneled on both sides, with a ½ inch cement asbestos board in the middle. The middle board, very strong, held the whole thing together. The old pine facings were bolted to the door. The bolts were so arranged that either side could be completely burned off without the whole thing failing. The closures were in the concrete beneath the door. The doors, when open, were held by good-looking heavy brass hooks, in turn held by fusible links.

On the floor below, the bowling alley doors were standard steel-hinged fire doors.

This left perhaps the greatest problem of all. A very

important feature of the planned project was to be the bowling alley. This was to occupy the whole basement immediately below the auditorium. Bowling is far from a quiet sport. Billy was having nightmares about future concerts, plays or lectures when the bowling noise was so loud as to be disruptive.

Fortunately, the project got its first good break. Billy hired an especially good engineer because he previously hadn't done a building of this size. The engineer insisted on a concrete slab floor. The basement would house the furnace room. This was a considerable help for dampening sound transmission. Also, Billy was planning a bowling alley ceiling in separate segments so that each sloped enough to provide space for fluorescent lighting fixtures, which couldn't be seen by the bowlers or an audience. Billy suspended these by acoustical clips and provided heavy insulation. Also, several ducts beneath the stage received sound absorbing liners and were heavily sound insulated on the outside.

Later on, soon after the Community Center opened for business, a very philanthropic person, Betty Furness, gave it a gift of a chamber music concert by an excellent group. The concert was planned for an evening when the bowling alley would be in use. Billy, terrified, crept into the auditorium the night before. He could hear the bowling, but just barely. He hoped for the best. When the concert started the next night, even the quietest parts of the compositions drowned out the slight sound of pins. There was never a single complaint about the noise.

The Town Hall project was, for a time, going forward very well. But during the planning stages, someone threw a monkey wrench into the works. The American Legion had a good basketball team, which had been practicing and playing at a nearby local school gymnasium. This gymnasium was far from deluxe. The players conceived the idea of electing Charley Cushman, who was on the Community Center Board, their chairman and, through him, getting the entire project changed to building a gymnasium for their team. They also opted for having professional wrestling and boxing matches there.

The basketball court and the spectator space they wanted would require a much larger building than planned. When faced with the higher cost, they argued for a cheaply built structure with no money wasted on the design or the fine points of the building. Charley Cushman, feeling important as both the chairman of the Legion committee and a member of the Community Center Board, argued long and hard for the basketball facility. Billy pointed out that, although they had a successful team now, they had never had one before and probably wouldn't again. Furthermore, the building would be substantially wasted except in basketball season. Billy argued that Middleburg was a charming little town and the projected Community Center would add to its charm, whereas the basketball building would be a large eyesore and probably draw a less desirable type of person to the town.

A controversy raged. Construction was stopped on the building. The excavation had been done and the foundations were already in place. While the decision was being made, it felt to Billy that the future of the town was weighing in the balance.

It was finally decided to continue with Billy's design. The name of the facility was changed from "The Town Hall" to "The Community Center."

Not long afterwards, a large unified high school was built at the county seat. There was a fine big gymnasium with a beautiful basketball court.

Within the next few years, Billy built nine structures in Middleburg. The town became famous. Two presidential candidates, Kennedy and Reagan, lived in the immediate vacinity. Ambassadors and military brass bought places nearby. Billy now and again wondered what would have happened had they built the shabby basketball building.

As the building neared completion, Billy and the Jacksons went to it almost daily, picking color schemes, selecting furniture, even designing the large table for the director's room. Billy insisted on finishing the old pine very lightly, with only wax, and it turned out beautifully. The Jacksons sent Billy to New York to pick the stage curtains and the two-story-high curtains for the main room.

Finally, there was a big bash on opening night. The guests assembled in the large room, but controversy was not over. The room looked exquisite with the soft green curtains closed. It was late May and a warm evening. There was to be a very short ceremony and then a party. The ceremony was slightly late in starting. As the capacity crowd of guests sat in the new chairs, the temperature began to rise. The windows on both the first and second floors were open, but not a breath of air penetrated the heavily lined and interlined curtains. Out of respect for Dorothy Jackson, no one dared open the curtains. Finally, a famously headstrong lady, Miss Charlotte Noland, the owner and principal of an ultra successful prep school, Foxcroft, and a member of the old Southern aristocracy, got up and opened them. The audience applauded. Cool air streamed through the windows.

The building and grounds, both outside and in, had turned out sensationally. Although the project was for all the people, it turned out that most of the party guests were of the financial elite. To Billy's infinite surprise, Kitty

Dudley sought him out, grabbed him, and kissed him.

"Billy, it's gorgeous," she said.

Charley Cushman, as a member of the board, was there in all his glory. Forgotten was the basketball controversy.

CHAPTER 15

It happened that, during the nineteenth century, many young industries were springing up in the United States: railroad, steel, oil, and many others. Some of these grew on the backs of thousands of immigrants. Many large fortunes were made then and an aristocracy of new wealth created. By the mid-twentieth century, some of the beneficiaries of this were making their way to Middleburg. Some of these, attracted by the sporting life, were amongst the more obstreperous variety.

One of these was Howard Paul. Financially, his credentials were of the best. Actually, he was a tragic character. Due to a childbirth injury, he was terribly handicapped. He was a powerful man, all of his great strength being in his arms and shoulders. He could walk without help, but with a terrible halt in his stride. To make it worse, he had a brother who was a great athlete, polo player, and social success. Someone said that nature had been very unkind to Howard, that he considered the best defense was an offense, and acted accordingly. Also, he frequently sought solace in liquid nourishment.

On one of these occasions, he called Billy, who had been making some sketches for him, and said he wanted to have a conference. There had been a severe thunder storm, and all the lights were out. Howard, very drunk, was seated at a table in his rather attractive old country house. For light, he had a small lamp on the table.

Billy sat down and they began to talk. Howard was making sweeping gestures with one arm. Soon the arm hit the chimney of the little lamp and knocked it off the base. The oil was in the base, but the end of the wick was attached to the chimney. It was still lighted. Unfortunately, the other end of the wick was still in the base with the oil. Billy saw the flame slowly working down the wick toward the oil. He made a pass toward separating the two.

"That's alright, Billy. That won't hurt anything; leave it alone."

Billy desisted. The flame got closer and closer. In desperation, Billy said, "Isn't that a roof leak in the other room?" Howard gazed at it, and Billy disconnected the wick.

The maid brought Howard another drink and one for Billy. Howard launched into a fantastic and, Billy thought, entirely fanciful story of certain claimed recent misbehavior of his own. He also started directing Billy to show absolutely impossible things on the drawing. Luckily, a protracted phone call took Howard into a different room for some time. Billy simply left the house and drove away.

One day soon afterward, Howard summoned Billy to his office in Warrenton. This had a rather cheap old desk, some serviceable chairs, an old rug on the floor, 17 photos of his stable, three of his horses, a photo autographed by Warren Harding and one by Woodrow Wilson, and an original Gilbert Stewart painting.

"I think my paper needs some cartoons, huh? They're nice to look at, huh, and people notice them. What I want is, huh, all the hounds around, and the M.F.H. is Patton, and the mask is Adolf Hitler. And then it says, 'The next event' and shows Tojo as a fox in flight followed by the whole pack. Can you draw that up for me?"

"I've never done a cartoon, but I'd love to try."

Billy was very interested and put his whole heart and soul into it. Several people saw it and thought it was wonderful.

Howard Paul had several properties in the hunt country. (It was a cousin of his who had created Paul Plaza in Palm Beach.) The properties included an attractive old house six or eight miles from Middleburg, a stud farm near there, and an office and residence in Warrenton, another small town.

Early one afternoon, Billy, by appointment, with the cartoon, parked his little convertible in front of Howard's house in Warrenton. There was a long concrete walk from the old iron gate to the house. The front door of the house was below grade; there were several steps down to it. The first floor was entirely on concrete slabs. Howard's wife, Sarah, an entertaining person, and her younger brother's attractive wife, Kathy, were living there. The brother was still away with the Marines.

As Billy made his way, carrying the cartoon, along the concrete front walk, Kathy appeared at the door: "Billy, come quick." Howard, very drunk, was walking around in circles. Kathy was afraid he would fall and fracture his skull on the concrete floor.

Billy waited until the right moment and body-blocked him onto the sofa. Kathy disappeared. In a few moments, she was back, pale as a sheet. "I just called the doctor and asked how many sleeping pills I could give Howard. He said not more than one. "My God, I just gave him three in his drink."

Howard quickly subsided on the sofa and was out cold for several hours.

The cartoon had, for safety, been concealed in a closet.

The ladies regaled Billy with the horrors of the morning. Howard had awakened with a hangover and to relieve it, started drinking. By mid-morning, he was thoroughly drunk and in a mean mood.

He started walking down to his office. On the way, he got into three fights. He was running for the state house of representatives and some of his supporters, as damage control, succeeded in getting him off the street and back home. (Because of his enormous financial advantage, he had done fairly well in politics).

Once home, Kathy and Sarah had to cope with him. The knock-out pills had relieved the situation for a while. They thought they could get a guard from the mental hospital that had "dried him out" before to come and keep him quiet that night.

Billy's arrival was a great help to them. He agreed to stay for dinner, and presumably the guard would arrive somewhat afterward. During dinner, they received a phone call from the mental hospital. They could not send a guard; the only one available had done it before and was too afraid of Howard to come.

Around this time, Howard began to waken. They could hear him in the next room carrying on an imaginary conversation: "I love you, baby, the Lord knows I love you, baby."

Billy simply didn't want to go home and leave Kathy and Sarah all alone to cope with Howard. "I'll stay tonight and do anything I can to help you," he said. "You can't possibly cope with Howard. He's 50 percent bigger than you are and twice as strong. I won't possibly get in a fight with him. That's no way to handle him anyhow. Actually, I'm sorry for Howard. He has a terrible handicap in life. If I can help you, I'll be glad to try."

The truth was this seemed pretty chancy. The relief on their faces was striking though.

As Howard revived more, the situation worsened. First, food kept him temporarily occupied. Then Billy was able to distract him with conversation about the house and Howard's own idea about changing the entrance.

They started looking around at things and soon got to a side door, which, like the front door, was below grade, with a small retaining wall around it and steps up to the grass. Howard started disagreeing with Billy about everything. Soon he said, "Want to fight?"

"No, I don't want to fight, Howard," Billy answered.

"I'm going to beat the hell out of you, but I can't roll up my sleeves. Will you roll up my sleeves for me?"

Billy rolled up Howard's sleeves, while realizing that the terrain, down in this pit, was the most unfavorable for him if he actually let it come to blows.

As he finished, he was aware of Kathy standing just inside the screen door. She threatened Howard.

Howard was now completely confused by Billy's lack of resistance.

"Howard, I've almost finished that cartoon about Patton, Hitler, and Tojo. I'll bring it over next time I come." He did not tell him it was actually already finished and there in a closet, as Billy did not want him to be able to deface it.

Billy never found out whether Kathy had slipped Howard another Mickey Finn, but his rage began gradually to subside. Before long he sat down, wrote something, and with a grandiose gesture, handed Billy a check for $500, with no explanation. (Billy, having sent Howard no bill, soon returned the check).

A very stressful hour or two passed, but finally Sarah was able to get Howard upstairs and to bed. She had to call Billy to help him get back from the bathroom. Billy, with an enormous effort, had to practically sling him onto the bed. This apparently annoyed him, but, whether because of the Mickey Finn or simple exhaustion, he couldn't get up. Once more, he said, "Want to fight?"

"No, I don't want to fight."

Billy let it go at that. He retreated to his room, locked the door, and, thankfully, went to sleep.

CHAPTER 16

Due to the great influx of Northern wealth in the twentieth century, the social, and even in part, the political control of Middleburg had passed to the Northerners. There were still, however, various survivors of the old Southern aristocracy. They were frequently dead broke. One of these was Samuel Wilson. When he was a baby, about six months old, his mother had been burned to death when her own clothing caught fire. Sam had never been quite normal.

Due to his love of flying, Sam had become a friend of Billy's. Before WWII, at age 19, he had married a rich Canadian divorcee, Leslie Gans, 26, and the daughter of B.B. Gans. He was head of Gans Motors, Canada's largest motor manufacturers. Leslie had given him a Luscomb "Silvair," a very nice little two-passenger plane. Billy had a number of flights with him in it. Sam was trying to get enough hours in the air to try for co-pilot on Pan-Am. He succeeded in this, and by the time of Pearl Harbor, he had a regular flying job. By V.E. day, he was a first captain.

After the war, Sam resigned his Pan-Am job and started an air field in Miami. This did scintillantly well at first. The money from the "Earney Pile Bill" enabled veterans to study almost anything they wanted free of charge. Many chose flying. Sam's flying lessons venture was flourishing.

Disaster ensued when the "Earney Pile" money ran out.

Sam had now lost his seniority at Pan-Am. He was soon back near Middleburg trying to make do on a farm he had inherited. Money was not a problem because of Leslie's family money; however, Sam drank under pressure. When working for Pan-Am, the regular hours and the constant obligation to be sober had kept him away from the bottle.

It happened one day that Billy, on the way to a routine inspection of a project, stopped for gas. He saw Sam there, who said, "Why don't you come with me? I'm going over to Winchester to try out an airplane. I may buy it. If I do, we might take a trip somewhere in it."

After a wild ride in the plane, Sam landed and invited Billy to dinner to discuss the trip. The evening ended with plans to go hunting in Canada. Billy was to find the best place to go.

The wildlife and tourist services were the best places to start. Several of them sent Billy letters, pamphlets, and pictures. One of them, from Ontario, seemed outstanding.

"In the autumn most of the ducks and geese who have nested in eastern Canada and the Arctic migrate down the shores of Hudson Bay and into James Bay, where thousands of them gather on the rich marshes, and stay until the first real winter storm drives them to start their long flight south," Billy told Sam.

There was also a pamphlet from the Hudson's Bay Company, offering to take hunters out from Moose Factory at Moosenee at the mouth of the Moose River to shoot on the marsh at Partridge Creek. Even these names thrilled Billy, as did the seventeenth-century British flag logo on Hudson Bay's letters. There was no problem in deciding that this would be the trip.

Sam didn't buy the plane, but he had a good station

wagon, which took all of their gear and enabled them to cross the border at Niagara Falls. Sam had great admiration for his father-in-law whom he called "The Old Man." On the long drive to Canada, the conversation frequently turned to him.

Sam said he had shown him all through his main plant one day. He'd stopped and chatted with many of the workers, all of whom seemed to like him. One of them still called him by his first name. Long ago, they had worked together on the assembly line. The Old Man seemed to know all about every part of the plant and loved it all.

Their route took them not far from his house, and Mr. Gans called him from customs and made an engagement to come by his house later that evening. Luckily, Billy advised Sam that they should get a room in a motel and not count on spending the night there unless invited.

Promptly at 8:00, as planned, they arrived at Mr. Gans' place, a large, more or less French nineteenth-century-style edifice. Mr. Gans was cordial, but he soon turned to one of his daughters and said, "Emily, take Mr. Dew out to the billiard room; I want to talk to this boy."

The rather attractive girl and her date provided Billy a pleasant evening, told him what they could about Canada and duck shooting, and finally led him back to the grand salon.

Sam looked like a wilted cabbage. While they were leaving, Mr. Gans told Billy good-bye with hospitable cordiality. He was rather stern with Sam, but there was a real tone of affection, and disappointment, in his voice as he said good-bye to him.

As they drove away, it was obvious that Sam had been through the ringer. "After we called up, the Old Man called Leslie, who was in Florida, to learn why we had come to

Canada without her. It's true that we have been drinking too much, but she stretched the truth pretty far. She said I'd pushed her out of the car while it was still running, that I'd slapped her, that I'd made her life pure hell. She said she'd had to go to Florida to get away from me."

The Old Man said this simply couldn't go on, and said a separation would be in order. He also chewed Sam out pretty thoroughly in general.

Sam had simply idolized his father-in-law and took the incident hard. Through much of the night, Billy was aware that Sam was up writing something. It was a letter to Mr. Gans, written in a manner that Billy thought semi-insane, claiming great virtues for himself with no relation whatsoever to reality.

Billy was afraid that Sam would take to the bottle. Nevertheless, in the morning they pushed on north. The work of driving the small station wagon, the sight of the northern towns, and the increasing wildness of the country seemed to divert Sam's attention from his troubles. As they crossed the north-south divide, it was snowing. This introduced a little more adventure, since they would be camping out at Partridge Creek.

The end of the road came at Cochrane, Ontario, a town with unpaved streets, a large general store, and wonderful grouse shooting in the area. The only transportation to Moosenee was the Ontario and Northlands Railway, which the province had built in a very unsuccessful effort to make Moosenee a seaport.

This railroad was, in itself, something to remember. Its main function now was to carry pulp wood and hunters to Moosenee during shooting season and a few supplies to the James Bay area. On board with Billy and Sam was the Episcopal bishop of the Arctic, several school teachers, a dozen or so hunters, several Cree Indians, the game warden, and two Mounties. Sam and Billy soon knew everyone on the train. There were no towns along the way, but once in a while the train would stop to deliver something to someone along the track.

At one stop, the engineer came back to visit with the passengers leaving the fireman to run the train. He had a nice chat with Billy and Sam, and hospitably invited them up into the engine, which was wood-burning. The cab was clean and a fairly pleasant place to ride. At least, this was an unusual experience.

Billy finally asked how to get back to the cars. "Oh, you want to go back. I'll slow the train and you can get off and hop on the car when it comes along."

In Moosenee, the Hudson's Bay Company proved efficient but hardly deluxe. There was an old pickup truck to carry hunters from the station to the dock. One could sit fairly comfortably on one's sleeping bag in the back of this. At the dock was a nice big Hudson's Bay canoe with an outboard for the half-hour trip to Moose Factory Island.

On the island were the large, warm, comfortable Hudson Bay staff houses, where one slept and had fairly good meals. There was also the large trading post store, where one bought all food and supplies for the four-day trip to Partridge Creek.

The weather had now worsened and there was about six inches of snow on the ground. Furthermore, the forecast was not good, but Sam and Billy weren't about to turn back. Their little party, which was comprised of themselves, two Cree guides, and everything they needed for four days on the marsh, were all packed into the canoe. (This type of canoe, prevalent in the far north, was much larger than the familiar type in the States. Fortunately, it was a great deal more seaworthy.)

Their objective, Little Partridge Creek, was completely frozen at its mouth. However, several miles up in the woods, the creek (actually a small river) split into two streams. They returned to Big Partridge, went through the snow-covered woods to the division point, and came back down to the nice camp site. They had bought a small tent for Sam and Billy, one for the guides, and another for meals.

When the guides said the tents were ready, they entered theirs. Billy said, "This is the Ritz." There were two folding cots, each with their mattresses, two racks of local large sapling trunks, neat spruce bows covering the floor, and a small gasoline stove.

The stove, a great luxury, was also a mixed blessing. The junior guide, Allen Cheechoo, came to light it every morning when the time came for them to get up. It was at the end of the tent used for passage. Each morning, Allen set the tent on fire trying to start it, and each morning there would be furious, successful attempts to beat out the fire.

There was also a separate tent for the guides and one for meals, this being the main tent. It was there that Sam became a great hero for declaring his family's connection with the motor car company.

A group of Canadians, who would usually have been camped some distance away, were very close because of the weather. Their chief guide, Jim Cheechoo, was the uncle of the boy who set the tent afire every morning. Billy and Sam had already been up to see them. They were a fortunate group. Their main actor seemed to be a Mr. Brown, a handsome, tall Canadian, who owned, amongst other things, some fishing cabins back home.

The terrible weather was also excellent for shooting. There were geese everywhere. By the end of the second day, Billy and Sam had bagged their limits.

The weather continued to get worse. Mr. Brown came by and said Jim was going to make them go back early the next day. All night long, the geese flew over getting a start for their trip to the Gulf coast. There was a high wind blowing. The geese made such a racket that Sam and Billy could hardly sleep. It was very cold.

Early the next morning, Jim came by and made it final—they were going back. The only question was—by sea or by land? They could have huddled there and waited to be sent for by sled from Moosenee, or have gone down to the beach and tried to force their way across the rapidly freezing edge of the bay ice. Billy wanted to go back cross-country by sled. The only thing was the canoes were all packed and ready.

It was decided that they should go to the beach and try to make it. The Canadians left first. Billy and Sam were finally put snugly in the canoe. That meant that they were completely under the cover of the large tarpaulin. At the rear was just enough room for George Cary, their guide, and at the very front room for Allen Cheechoo. It was not long before Billy also stuck his head up past the waterproofing.

It was well that he did. Along the shore were tracks of animals: moose, bear, wolves, all of which had been there since the snow had started. When they got to the place where the rivers became one, Allen got his rifle ready. As they turned into the larger stream, he was poised for a shot. Up and down, as far as the eye could see, there was no game in the river.

However, on the beach things were better. The Canadians had given Jim three shells and asked him to get them three geese. Jim quickly disappeared into the mist, which was much thicker near the water. Before long, he was back with three geese. They had also put up a shelter from the wind, which was stronger here.

Before long, there was a lull, and Jim said they might "try it." Jim's canoe started first. As Billy and Sam's canoe was readied, Billy, for the first time on the trip, was really scared. There was still some time before they reached the large waves at the edge of the ice. Jim's canoe with one more person aboard got stuck. They didn't stop; it was every canoe for itself. They pushed away and were soon in the midst of large waves. One wave hit them wrong and Billy thought they were going over.

The sea was now getting calmer. It seemed that the rough waves were at the edge of the ice. He asked George Cary about this. "You see that storm in the distance? If that gets to us, we're in trouble. If we can beat it to the river, we're alright."

The tide was in their favor. All the way in from the Atlantic, through Baffin Bay, Hudson Bay, and all the way to the very end of James Bay and into the Moose River, it kept coming. It seemed to sweep them into the river, and right to their dock.

They also found that Jim Cheechoo had somehow become disentangled from his trap and was on his way in, complete with his Canadians. They never understood how.

On the way home, Sam became unbearable. He had, whether he realized it or not, married Leslie hoping to become successful, rich, and prominent. He hadn't stopped to think that his Southern blood line was good.

Despite the changes in Sam's life, Billy and he remained friends once Billy helped him realize what a perfectly beautiful trip they had had. They went quail hunting not long after their return. Billy had ten geese and distributed them around to various friends, along with perfectly flabbergasting stories of the unusually early storm and cold, which had struck them in Moosenee.

CHAPTER 17

Billy had a problem: to find work. Howard's unfortunate divorce from Sarah provided some.

During WWII, some of the British children (of the very highest classes) had been brought over to America for safety's sake. Some of them were parked at the Paul's house on Long Island.

Howard was not one to be caught off guard by things like this. On his very best behavior, he buzzed around considerably. Lady Gweneth Parks-Bowles was, at sixteen, the oldest and very pretty. Howard was duly fascinated. In her company, he toned down his lifestyle and behaved decently. His mother was surprised. His father, who really knew him better, was astounded.

All this was during the war. However, wars do end. Several months after V-E day, Gweneth and two younger sisters left for England, and it wasn't long after that Howard did too.

Gweneth's place was grandiose and handsome. In the early sixteenth century in England, it had happened that a certain Swedish princess had arrived with her eyes on Henry VIII. She didn't make it (Henry was looking toward Spain), and went back to Sweden. However, her first lady in waiting did much better. She fell in love with a certain

Englishman, and they were married. He built her a castle using the three-sided Swedish plan. Located only a few miles from Salisbury, it looked very good, nestled down beside the river.

Early in the next century, Gweneth's ancestor bought it. It was now full of Velasquezes, Titians, Reynolds, el Grecos and many others. Howard soon made himself at home there. Billy only knew that sometime thereafter he and Gweneth returned to America as husband and wife.

Howard looked wonderful. One of his orations was, "The butler built me up. The first night he said: 'Your Lordship, dinner is served.'"

Howard wanted to move back to his place near Middleburg. He was considering building a full-size addition to his home. Once more, he was on the phone to Billy.

Howard's house had already been done over by a fairly good, but not certified, architect from Warrenton.

In front it sloped up to a design, which Billy thought fairly good, although completely different from his own style. He wanted to keep this, but respected Howard's wish to have it rise to second-floor height separately.

Everything was fine until Howard went to see Williamsburg. Oh, those cute little houses! The chance of keeping the wing reasonably matching the main part was now gone. Billy did his best, but Howard was insistent that the Williamsburg style was vastly superior to that of the house.

While under construction, things got better. Billy received an invitation to a sleigh-riding party there. His partner was to be an old friend of Gweneth's from England. The course was also of interest: a long slope, beginning where the new wing was to be and extending far down the hill. Also, whereas every American schoolchild has a wooden sled, the enormous and strong tin trays from the Paul's kitchen were the "sleds" of choice there.

Billy had, naturally, never seen Jane Cummings. His first glance fixed that. She was one of the prettiest girls he could remember. She also liked sleigh riding. They both boarded a large tray and slid to the bottom of the hill; each time was another chance for Billy to put his arms around this English vision. Finally, they were called inside for cider and fresh salmon sandwiches.

Billy still did the best he could with the addition. Gweneth offered him coffee each time he came. They would sit in her new studio, drink the coffee, and discuss everything from sleigh riding to England.

Billy was surprised to hear Gweneth say that when she was a child, she never really knew her parents, and she was rather scared to death of them. Every Sunday evening, if her parents were not doing anything else, she and her sisters would be invited to have supper with them. Gweneth's father, the Earl of Reming, was to them a thrilling monster. At these Sunday night parties, he would reign supreme, asking them terrifying questions and frighten them half to death.

It turned out that Jane was in love with Peter Wright, who was with Jake Jenning's company and who was soon in charge of their New York office. This little bit of gossip reached Billy and may have saved him a bundle.

CHAPTER 18

Billy now considered himself a master of the art of practicing residential architecture. He understood the value of a proper social circle in obtaining jobs. He had even been invited to a considerable number of parties. He began to think of returning these invitations. On one trip back to Sweet Briar to see his mother, Billy had a long talk with an old friend, the violin teacher, Ernest Ziechiel, who told him that he certainly must.

So, on one fine day in late August, the invitations began to roll. He invited everyone who had invited him to their gatherings, many people with whom he had worked, plus a few others. Billy reserved the Community Center. His objective was to actually have it on the part of the outdoor stage, which ran out past the building on the right hand side. He had everything figured out, including the correct amount of food and drink.

On the day of the party, the weather seemed perfect, not a cloud in the sky. Billy was there very early, and he was worried. He had no idea what would happen. The invitations said 5 p.m., the going hour at the time. Five o'clock came, and there were no guests. Five-ten came, and still not a soul. Five-fifteen, and then one person. Five-twenty, and then a group arrived. Finally, almost everyone he had invited and a few extras simply appeared.

The early autumn sun was streaking beautiful light across the theater. That soon faded and there was a beautiful twilight. Then night fell and the party still roared.

It was almost midnight when Billy finally had paid all the bills, tipped everyone, and gone home. It had been a fine experience for him, and he couldn't imagine another year when he would not have another party.

Billy also loved dove shooting. After his party, it happened one day that someone invited him to shoot with them. For doves one should be in the field early in the afternoon. (Morning shooting is illegal.) There should be enough people so that every part of the field has a gun ready. Usually ten or fifteen people will suffice.

Dove shooting was not easy. The birds twisted and turned, frequently came from behind or from a side not being watched. Billy "hung in there," and finally got his limit of twelve.

He was invited several more times and never declined. From then on, this was one of his favorite sports. For years he kept it up, almost never failing to get the twelve doves. A number of his clients also loved it. One day, he was invited to two shoots. He went to the first and got several doves without missing one. Then he went on to the next shoot. He finally missed one shot, but no more.

Every year, Billy would have the same party. It was always a huge success. It became famous. Between the party, dove shooting, tennis, and an interminable number of other people's parties to which he was invited, his autumns and early winters were fantastic. Once Billy was invited to three parties on the same afternoon, and he managed to get to all three.

In Warrenton, there was an older couple, Bill and Lou

Doellar, who also loved to shoot. They were also very well provided with this world's goods. Near Warrenton, their house was three stories high. It had a main room with columns that somewhat resembled palm trees. The other grand rooms were full of trinkets from all over the world. They spent the winters, however, on the eastern shore of Maryland. There they had two magnificent duck shooting places, one inland, the other right on the bay. In the one on the bay, they had gotten a very good artist to paint murals. They also had a table, which at breakfast contained almost everything that anyone could possibly want.

After breakfast, one would sally forth in a power boat, with guides, to a blind where one would find not only wonderful shooting (depending on the weather), but also Scotch, bourbon, and gin. There was also radio communication between the various blinds.

Also in Warrenton, there was a lovely old house named Dakota where Susan Hamilton, a beautiful divorcee, heiress, and great friend of the Doellar's lived. One day, Billy received a phone call from Lou Doellar inviting him to a duck shoot. She had difficulty in explaining to him how to find the place, but she then said, "Stop by Warrenton and bring Sue Hamilton." Billy was ecstatic.

He was careful at first not to overdo it. He objected strongly to some things Sue said. Finally, there was confusion as to which way they should go around Washington. Billy gave in to her route, using an excuse that he was confused, being unaccustomed to having such an attractive young lady in the car. From then on, things were fine.

At Honda River, there was an attractive group of people, not least of which was the Marquis de la Rochefoucauld, from France. He did not shoot, having only come for pleasure. Another evening Billy, idly discussing his long ago trip through France, mentioned the small hotel where he first stayed in Paris. The Marquis said he knew of it, that in the old days he used to keep his mistress there.

Billy was intent on the sport. One morning, he and Sue were quartered in a blind. There had not yet been any shooting, but a group of ducks was just "coming in." At this critical stage, when they were overhead, but just out of range trying to decide whether to come in and land amongst the decoys, Billy was down in the blind, hardly daring to even look at them. Sue screamed at him, "There's one," and pointed in the air. The group of ducks immediately headed for other places. She was severely chastised. However, the next time her behavior in the blind was excellent.

On the way home, they rendezvoused at one point with the Marquis. It was extremely cold. In their boat, Billy had his arm around Sue. There was a problem in keeping the Marquis warm. His French clothes didn't do the job. All they could do was exhort his boatman to hurry home.

The next morning it was colder still. The guides said they couldn't go out because the bay was frozen solid. Toward the end of the morning, the conversation referred to certain data, which was in Sue's room. Billy gleefully followed Sue to the room but scrupulously behaved himself while there. (He later very much regretted this.)

On the way back to Warrenton, Billy was depressed. It seemed all of the fun was over. Sue said she knew certain people in the area who had a particularly interesting house, and she would introduce him to them. They arrived in Warrenton at 6 o'clock, and Sue had an engagement for the evening, but Billy was firm in his idea of calling her up and making a dinner date.

In two or three days, however, Billy came down with a heavy cold. When he recovered, he realized some bad pains in his left hip had worsened. He went to Washington to see his doctor, Henry Ecker. Henry didn't say too much, but sent him to another doctor who x-rayed his back and then made a diagnosis.

Billy had two badly damaged vertebrae in his lower spine. The pain in his hip was simply horrible. He would probably have to have a spinal operation. Billy was sent to bed in the hopes of avoiding surgery. But no luck. He called Ecker and said, "If I have the operation, I would like to get the best surgeon, no matter where he lives or what he charges." Ecker called back in about an hour. "I got you Hugo Rizzoli."

The next afternoon, about 5 o'clock, Billy had another phone call from the Washington Hospital Center. "We have a room for you. You should be here by 6 o'clock." Middleburg is over an hour's drive from the hospital, and Billy wasn't about to take his own convertible for an unlimited stay in Washington. His draftsman, Jack Irvin, drove him in, arriving about 7 o'clock. Dinner there was at 6 o'clock. Billy had to wait to be admitted. When he finally got to his room, the nurse was only able to get him a sandwich out of the cash stand, which didn't improve his night. He was also hooked up to various pulleys and weights for tension.

Dr. Rizzoli came in the next day and examined him. If the tension and the rest didn't cure him, he would have the operation, he was told.

In the hospital, like many other places in Washington, there were many things left to be desired. The food was fairly good, some of the nurses fairly bad. After two weeks, Dr. Rizzoli, always conservative, decided complete bed rest and spinal tension weren't working, and Billy would have to have surgery.

The operation was to be July 5th. On the 4th, the anesthesiologist came and paid a long visit. After he left, about 10 o'clock, two nurses aides came in, a little over-friendly, with some bourbon, and insisted that Billy get drunk with them. Billy refused in no uncertain fashion. They kept insisting and became angry. Finally, they left. Billy realized that this was the 4th of July in Washington. At 12 p.m., the sign came up over his door, "Nothing by mouth."

The operation took about four hours. Back in his room, he was flat in his bed with the sides up high all around. His lunch arrived and someone to feed it to him. The person was called away because some victims of a traffic accident had arrived in the hospital. This left his lunch sitting on the high sides of his bed. Very shortly, however, Dr. Rizzoli arrived and quickly procured more help. In about 10 days, Billy was able to leave the hospital.

It had been a long hard pull, and he was glad it was over. Dr. Rizzoli had said Billy couldn't shoot that fall except with a 410-caliber gun. It happened that, some time before, he had seen a little double-barreled 410 in a gun store and liked it so much that he had bought it. He had never done much with it—just kept it as a beautiful toy. The first day of the season he was invited to a shoot and came with the very nice little Italian 410. When the shoot was over, he had his twelve doves. It also happened later that fall that he got permission to shoot quail on a client's land. He still had to use the 410. At the end of the shoot, he had his five, including two on the covey rise.

There was a charming family in Middleburg, the C. Oliver Iselins. Billy had frequently played tennis with them. One day, they were having a huge luncheon party. It was agreed that each man was to find a lady and take her as his partner when the luncheon was served. Sue was there, and Billy was very sure to invite her. However, when the time came, there was no Sue. Billy searched and searched.

Freda Burling was there; Billy was finding her very attractive and took her for the lunch. He enjoyed it immensely.

It also happened that there was a party in Washington called the Dancing Class. It was supreme, over and above anything else; it was always at the Sulgrave Club, always white tie, always with Mayer Davis in attendance. It happened three times every year, having started during World War I. John Logan, a prominent friend of Billy's, had been going to it for years as a bachelor. He had been guilty of un-bachelor-like behavior, however, as he had gotten married. He was therefore immediately dumped. Billy had also been playing tennis with the Harry Darlingtons. Harry was the son of Mrs. Garrett, who was on the ultra-select committee of the Dancing Class. Billy soon received an invitation to replace John. He had also recently met the Edward Burlings. They were also at the Iselin's party. She was also an unusually attractive young lady, and Billy invited her to go to the luncheon with him. He had a most enjoyable luncheon.

Before long came time for Billy's first dancing class. He arrived early, and viewed Freda Burling across the hall on the first floor before going to the entrance desk. He joined her for a chat.

After he went in, the festivities really started. There was Mayer Davis making beautiful music. Billy went through the line greeting Mrs. Garrett and the other three hostesses. Toward the right was a table with two bartenders dispensing very small drinks. He found out the reason for the size: in previous times some of the older ladies had "gotten stuck." They considered that by having the bar there, the possibility would exist for more dancers. Billy loved to dance; he loved the music. He danced several times with Freda Burling, at least once each with the members of the committee, and with everyone else whom he either knew or met there.

CHAPTER 19

There was in Middleburg a very old bank originally built by Will Hall, a well liked black contractor. Willy's father was Nate Hall, a wonderful old man, whose specialty was said to be singing orders to his men. Willy's son was trying to be an architect. The old bank was right on the central corner of the town opposite the Red Fox Tavern. It had four columns in front and was not a bad looking building. However, Middleburg was outgrowing it.

A group of men led by Duncan Read were planning a new one and invited Billy to be the architect.

The design Billy came up with, after negotiating a six percent commission, included the best brick (oversized and handmade) and the best detailing. The plaques had to be specially designed. A sculptor had to be found to make them from Billy's design. The transom over the front door was quite special and unlike any other anywhere.

At one point, Billy was absolutely paralyzed by the prospect that the bricks were not working out on the front elevation. However, the brick contractor simply said, "Leave it to me." When Billy next saw it, he was completely satisfied.

On the outside of the building, Billy was anxious to keep the front approximately flush, which left little room for a vestibule. The door faced northwest, the direction from which the worst storms came. Billy tried very hard to make a small vestibule. It finally passed. There was never a long enough line from the teller to the door to reach it.

In the basement were storage rooms, the employees' lounge, the director's room, and, in particular, a lock-up room right beneath the main security vault. In this room could be saved long-term valuables. Billy inherited valuable silver, and having no long-term residence, saved them there.

The director's room was carefully done. It had a large table with appropriate chairs. Its window was false. All the moldings were there, but behind it there was simply an illuminated picture.

Early in the construction, unfortunately, a spring developed in the foundation. Billy designed a sump pit with a water-operated sump pump to carry the water all the way to the city street behind the bank, which was at a considerably lower level.

Just before the bank opened for business, there was a meeting of the contractor, all the subcontractors, and Billy. They were to go through the building a room at a time. They started in the furnace room. The last one to come in shut the door. It couldn't be re-opened; the lock was defective. Phil Nelson, the contractor, was paranoid about being shut up underground. There was only one hope of getting out—one of the team was late. After 15 minutes or so, he appeared. Everyone yelled, "Don't shut the door." They were saved.

CHAPTER 20

At some time during World War II, a beautiful castle in Holland fell victim to an air raid. One night, the Mosquito bombers from England bombed it and killed the owner of the centuries-old estate. The deceased had been married to a rich Canadian whose brother was now president of the Iron Ore Company of Canada. His widow came back to this country and married Mr. Joseph Mulford. Mr. and Mrs. Mulford had a beautiful tennis court. Billy and others used to frequently play there. Pauline Betts Addie (Wimbledon Champion, 1949) gave lessons there once a week.

It happened that, one day, Mrs. Mulford told Billy that they were going to build a smaller home and wanted Billy to be the architect. They were tired of the large home, pool, and swim house, which they then had. Billy had also built a series of walls, where they had had only an unsightly enormous clay bank.

The new house was to be on the western part of their farm. Billy selected a site right where there was a line of trees, several hundred yards from the small country highway. The view was beautiful, so Billy ran the road through the trees and entered on the mountain side. Toward the view, he put a main living room, with largely glass walls, and a porch, and in the dining room a large bay window. There was also an attractive winding stairway. The walls of the house were stone.

The Mulfords never moved into the house. Through a series of events, it was bought by Jackie Mars of the chocolate company.

It happened that there was a serious recession. Billy had been "living high" and was seriously in debt.

Things started getting worse. He received a phone call from the president of the bank asking him to come to the bank and see him. The president ran over his account there and asked him to start curtailing it. Billy had no work in his office and simply couldn't do it. This was one of the worst times he could remember.

He could have gone along somewhat longer by selling his stocks, but they had already gone down so much that there hardly seemed any use doing so. He thought that if he could just keep them, their value would increase again.

Billy was greatly cheered when Bob Dodderidge called and asked him to design a house in the Caribbean at Palmas del Mar in Puerto Rico. The house was to be very long, but only 10 meters wide, the width of his lot. Further, the lot sloped 30 feet upward. Beyond that was a sheer cliff straight down to the sea.

The first thing required was a watercolor painting of it for the art committee. Billy hadn't done a watercolor in years and was no longer confident in his ability to do one. However, he immediately started work on it, sketching a bird's-eye perspective. (He had already worked out a rough plan.) His client said he could have three days to do it.

To draw the complicated plan in birds-eye perspective took almost a whole day. His client dropped by that afternoon and said, just as he was leaving: "I forgot to get my wife a Christmas present. I thought I would give her your sketch."

Billy was simply scared to death. He thought he could satisfy the art committee, believing they probably got only fair sketches from time to time, but to have something good enough to be framed and given to his clients seemed impossible. However, he started out. He worked as late as he could that evening and the next.

There was to be a parking place and a drying yard in the front; the parking was to be under the house, as well as the entrance. It was not an unusual arrangement in the area. A door led to an elevator up to the first and second floors. Above that were two bedrooms, with a deck over them. Beyond that was the third floor with one bedroom, a living room, and a bath. Beyond that was a patio with arches around it and a fountain in the middle. A small winding staircase rose to the portion of the roof, which had a trellis over it. Between the patio and the rear was a long room, which stretched the full length from side to side of the lot. Outside this room was another very small, irregularly shaped open patio, down three steps, filling the rest of the lot.

In Billy's office and his home were various watercolors he had made when in Europe years ago. Billy studied them carefully, hoping to regain his skills.

Billy kept watching the stock market. He was trying desperately to keep his stocks. One that he had, Itek, had been selling in the fifties and was now sinking like a lead balloon. He understood that if it stayed at five or more, it was safe. If it sank below that, he would get a margin call, which he couldn't meet. Every morning he checked the newspaper; the stock was still at five. This was for six or eight consecutive days. The market was still tumbling.

There came the third and final day on the picture. The arrangement was that Bob would come by for it at 3:30 and take it to be framed. Billy also had made out a bill for the entire amount owed him by then.

The moment finally arrived when Billy thought he could call the picture finished. He walked to the front of the office, and there was Bob ready to pick it up. Bob was more than delighted with the picture and also wrote Billy a check, which he immediately mailed to his stockbroker.

Billy had been taking long walks in the late afternoon. He couldn't keep his mind off his debts. Amongst other things, he felt disgraced. He had been gradually withdrawing sums from his stock account as he needed them. Each time he thought would be the last. It had finally gotten to him. (Two years later, Billy sold the Itek for exactly fifty dollars a share. He also soon sold others and wiped out his debt to his stockbroker.)

A little later, Billy's watercolor and his plans for the house in Puerto Rico proved successful. He had a wonderful time going up to the house site, taking the picture to show to the head of the art committee (who loved it), swimming, playing tennis, and driving around the country with his clients. In the evenings, they went to the club where there was a singer whom his clients' sons found most attractive. Early in the mornings, Billy and Henry, his clients' son, would go to the beach—a beautiful, broad, unbroken stretch, with wonderful palm trees at the end.

The Wimbledon tennis champion, Stan Smith, was there. He had recently married the beautiful and brilliant granddaughter of another client, John Logan, an old friend of Billy's in Middleburg. She had been undefeated in tennis in her four years at Princeton. He introduced himself to her, and both the Smiths were delightful.

The end of Billy's work finally came, and he boarded a plane for home. The financial crisis had wreaked its pitiful worst on the country but was now retracting vigorously. Billy's stocks were now coming back fast.

He had the plans for the Dodderidge's house almost finished. Bob would frequently come in and go over them and help arrange small details. During one visit, he dropped a bomb: he couldn't build the house. He had just heard from Puerto Rico that Palmas del Mar had lost so much money that they could no longer even put in the utilities for his place.

CHAPTER 21

The Dodderidge contract had been a godsend. Billy had no other work in his office. He moped around a few days, then thought of something else.

He had, years before, competed in the national competition for a memorial for a former great president: Franklin Delano Roosevelt. It had fascinated him. He read the particulars of the program one more time. He had always thought the committee was looking for something that leaned more toward landscaping than a building. The material said, "It suggests a more reflective expression and because of the location, a less dominant form than the Lincoln, Jefferson, and Washington Monuments. It will have its own quality, which will balance the three other monuments, and complete them."

Billy once again went down to the site. He noticed that the direction to the Lincoln Memorial, the Washington Monument, and the Jefferson Monument were not far from regularly spaced from the center point of his memorial. Why not have the whole thing open and develop these vistas? He also found that the line to the Unknown Soldier's Tomb and Mt. Vernon were similar. He thought he had it made. Even the slopes of the existing contours were favorable. There would be reflecting pools in each principal contour.

There would be large hedges, perhaps 25 feet high, beside the vistas and a very large one around the central court. In the exact center would be a large statue of President Roosevelt.

Originally, Billy's problem had been time. When the last day for submissions came, he had been far from ready. The last night, Billy and his assistant had worked until 5:30 in the morning, rested briefly, then worked again until 8 o'clock. It had been impossible to finish.

The winner of the first competition had been widely congratulated, but the press had a "field day" roasting it. Congress did not appropriate the money for it. A few years later, they hired another excellent large office to design it. The same thing happened again.

Billy had made a vow to finish his plan sometime, just for his own satisfaction. Years had gone by. Billy, struck by the recession, had once more nothing to do. He realized now was the time.

He agonized over what medium to use in the presentation. He still made trip after trip to the site studying every detail. He even knew where the little old Japanese light was that that country had given ours before World War II. In his design, he was careful to remove as few as possible of the Japanese Cherry trees.

Billy's design crystallized with a large central courtyard, which had a faint design in the floor. The walls of this were to be clipped hemlock. It was to be elliptical in shape, with the long axis perpendicular to the line from its center to the Washington Monument. This line ran a short distance to the Tidal Basin over which could be seen the monument, and it was embellished by hemlock hedges on both sides, but without pools.

The vista to the Lincoln Memorial was a great deal

longer, starting with two free-form pools. It was symmetrical as viewed from the large courtyard with several rectangular pools, somewhat narrower, along the way to the rising ground over which the Lincoln Memorial could be seen.

The vista to the Jefferson Memorial was much shorter but still longer than that to the Washington Monument. It also had two pools, identical to the other long axis, and still another short rectangular pool with a plaza beyond that. Over these, across the tidal basin, could be seen the Jefferson Memorial.

On the rear of the large plaza were two other vistas, one to the Tomb of the Unknown Soldier, the other in the direction of Mt. Vernon. These were much smaller vistas, and started with much smaller openings in the hemlock hedges. Immediately in the center of the rear of the large plaza, with only a very simple rounded top opening in the hedge, was a rose garden.

In the center of the main courtyard was to be a heroic statue of Franklin Delano Roosevelt. Around the periphery were several statues of common people of the day at much smaller scale than that of the president. There were also several high rectangular marble slabs engraved with carefully selected quotations from his speeches.

Billy resolved to select the best sculptor in the world. He thought the sculpture would determine the success of the memorial. These figures would have to show Roosevelt's hold on the people and their dependence on him.

Then came the staggering task of showing the memorial on canvas. He had decided to do it lightly in oils. At the top of his sheet was a cut through the large central plaza showing the main statue and the Washington Monument in the distance across the tidal basin. Below that was a large view showing the vista to the Lincoln Memorial with all the pools and landscaping of the memorial. He had decided to have additional Japanese cherry trees, identical to the famous ones already there, and, in addition, several other varieties, arranged so as to make a great show after the Akebono had lost their bloom. Scattered through these were very large box bushes, whose foliage greatly enhanced the appearance of the cherries. There were also to be many other flowering plants to prolong the show all summer.

On either side of the large view of the Lincoln Memorial were to be two much smaller squares, one containing a view of the vista to the Jefferson Memorial, the other of the view of the main plaza from the direction of the Lincoln Memorial. Beneath these, on one side, would be a young white woman with two children; on the other would be a black group. They were both gazing at their hero, Roosevelt.

It still remained for Billy to relearn the art of painting. Since WWII he had done virtually nothing except the Dodderidge picture, and, long ago, the Red Fox Tavern sign. The upper section, as wide as the picture at 4 feet, wasn't hard to lay out; but the other one—almost 3 feet-by-2 feet 6 inches high—was extremely difficult. It was a bird's-eye view. He put a large piece of tracing paper over it and kept trying. He had to succeed. It not only had to be in perspective but also to complete the plan in the picture.

Billy had already done a rear view of the statue, with great difficulty. So he started barely beyond that and showed everything, including the pools, the cherry trees, the box bushes, the hedges—everything until the Lincoln Memorial. The two groups of the statuary were also quite difficult. He had to get the correct expression on the faces.

After about three months of intense work, Billy

thought it was finished. Just about that time, he read in the morning paper that there had been a little publicized group of large, well known architects and landscape architects invited to each separately submit their plans for it, and that one had won it.

According to the rules of professional ethics, there was nothing Billy could do about this. He was now completely out of the picture.

From then on, one whole side of his office had only one decoration: his design for the Franklin Delano Roosevelt Memorial.

Freda Burling liked Billy's design and told him she would introduce him to anyone in Washington who could help him with his problem. Billy, however, was afraid to try. He had not seen the winning plans and thought they might be terribly good. For the rest of his life, however, he was sorry he hadn't pursued the matter.

CHAPTER 22

There was a couple Billy knew, Mr. and Mrs. Smith Bowman, in an adjoining county. Mrs. Bowman was the great-granddaughter of one of the most famous and beloved of earlier Americans, Robert E. Lee. The Bowmans wanted to move.

The land wasn't a large problem. There were lots available not far from their present home. The problem was, where should they move? They had been happy in their house with a privacy wall all around it enclosing a large, beautiful garden. A porch surrounded three sides of the house. It was 10 feet wide and had good looking wrought-iron railings.

Billy had known for some time that they might build a new house and was doing everything he could think of to try to get the contract. According to professional ethics at the time, he couldn't simply ask them for it and didn't think it would really help anyhow to do that.

At one party at the Community Center in Middleburg, the Bowmans and the Burlings were both there. Freda Burling took Billy to the Bowmans and said, "Here is Billy Dew, our favorite architect. If you build a house, he's the one to get."

Finally one morning, a call came from Mr. Bowman

asking Billy to come see him. He offered him the job. The house was to be Palladian style on a pretty lot near the river. But there was a problem with the lot. Mr. Bowman owned the entire lot to the river, but there was already a house on it. The Palladian house he wanted would have to be put on one side of the lot in order to have a view of the river. Beyond the house the contours were unsuitable.

The next Sunday morning, Billy was in his office working feverishly on the plan. The phone rang. It was Mr. Bowman. He had received an offer of another lot and wanted Billy to come in and see it. The lot was a dream. One could see the river, down the river, across the river, and up the river. It was two hundred feet above the river, forested with large oaks, hickory, poplar, and maple. A steep precipice led down to the river. Billy told Mr. Bowman to make every effort to get the property.

He would never forget that morning: clear, sunny, and mild. Mr. Bowman, because of his arthritis, stayed at the top, and Mrs. Bowman and Billy walked down to the brink of the precipice. The river was a beautiful green color with white where it flowed over rocks.

The Bowmans were just leaving for a short trip to Nantucket Island. Billy received a postcard from them in which they said, "We have decided that we would rather have French style than Palladian."

Billy at first felt doomed. But the word "French" in architecture has various meanings. He ran over the different styles in France, everything from Romanesque to post-le-Corbusier, and picked Louie XIV. In many ways, it was like Palladian without Palladian's very high ceilings which would not have made sense in an air-conditioned building. Their general look would finally be his.

Billy also considered that none of the British, neither

Lord Burlington nor the Earl of Westmoreland, had been able to really do a top-notch job on copying the French. He stretched the Louis XIV style a little in keeping curved passages with pilasters on both sides leading out to small buildings. One side contained a luxurious bedroom and the other a tiny apartment for the help.

The house required a large living room, a dining room, a library, a staircase to the basement, a powder room, a pantry, a large coat room, a kitchen, a servants' dining room, a small apartment for the help, two guest bedrooms, two baths, and a large porch, similar to the one in their former house. There was to be a winding staircase to the second floor. The second floor was smaller than the first with a very large bedroom, an upstairs living room, two baths and dressing rooms, and one additional room with a small bath. Also included was a large linen closet and a small one on the first floor.

The porch at first was a problem. Billy decided to have it open, around 20 feet wide for parties. It would be a little longer than the house and go around the corners. For winter use or stormy days, there would be at each end an octagonal porch, all glass on the side toward the view. In the basement was to be a five- or six-car garage, storage area, and various other things.

All of these things had to be fitted into Billy's exterior conceptual idea and into the ideas of his clients. This wasn't easy, but it had to be done, and Billy did it. The winding stairway curved over the front door, ran horizontally there, and continued its climb beyond. This room was a full two stories and had to have enough light. Immediately beyond was the living room. Beyond that was the broad terrace. To the right was the dining room, the pantry, the kitchen, the servants' dining room and apartment, and the porch.

To the left stood the library, the porch, two bedrooms with their closets, baths, and linen closet. There was also a large coat room, a powder room, and a small office.

Billy still had an enormous debt at the bank. As soon as checks should arrive from the Bowmans, he would deposit them.

The Bowmans were a nice couple. At Princeton, Mr. Bowman had studied architecture, and his first job had been in the field. Then, his father was so busy at their liquor distillery that he had left his job and gone home to help him with most admirable results. In addition, they owned an enormous amount of acreage where they had grown corn for their mash. The price of real estate had risen enormously in the area. It appeared that they should sell their property and seek other land. In addition, a group of people sought to build a planned town, Reston. It appeared that the Bowmans' land was just the place for them. The planners offered the Bowmans many times the value for it. There was nothing to do but sell.

Billy was, at first, frightened by the prospect of doing the interior. He could probably design it, but where would he get the complicated sixteenth-century French moldings, panels, and other things made? His problems faded away when Mr. Bowman pulled out a copy of *Great Georgian Houses*, showed him the doorway to the stair hall at the Hamilton house in Maine and said he wanted exactly that. This made Billy realize that interior would be, instead of Louis XIV, early American. He continued to design it that way. All principle rooms must have cornices, medallions, and perhaps dentiles or the equivalent. Every room was completely designed, all four sides, at ½-inch scale. No effort was spared to keep all parts of them in perfect scale.

Mrs. Bowman had chosen an old friend as the interior

decorator. Billy took a dim view of this, not expecting a good result. He soon saw that he was wrong. In the dining room, for instance, there was to be special paper on the wall prepared in New York. It showed various birds in trees, but the whole thing was so beautiful and so in keeping with the design of the house that it was amazing. He had seen various Chinese hand-painted wallpapers, but he had never seen anything like this. Throughout the house, the colors on the walls, the new furniture and the rugs were exceptional.

Walnut was selected for the wood, which was to be in "natural finish," such as the stairway and many of the cornices, windows, and floors, as well as the entire library.
The most important interior door was in the exact middle of the house, from the entrance hall to the living room. This, like many of the very early nineteenth-century houses, had a glass overdoor, divided into smaller sizes with wooden muntins, in a typical eighteenth-century pattern. When it was finished and installed, it was beautiful. Everyone, including the workmen, on the job, loved it. However, Mr. Bowman didn't like it and ordered it removed and replaced by a large plain arch. Billy understood why he didn't like it. The two arches imitated from the pictures of the one in Maine (they were on both sides of the entrance hall) were more impressive. Billy had worked very hard on all three, and felt satisfied that he had reached the best solution. He tried hard to persuade Mr. Bowman, but to no avail. He had no choice but to relay Mr. Bowman's direction to the men.

They were so reluctant to do it that they made every possible excuse to postpone. They finally trumped up some reason to dismiss it. Mr. Bowman finally agreed. "I lost that one."

Finally, the entire project was finished. All the roads were in; the landscape was finished. The swimming pool was complete, as were all the terraces toward the river. The house itself was beautiful.

Billy received a phone call from another prominent man asking him to design a house. It would also be in McLean, also in the French. It was on a several-acre lot, but without any magnificent view. The view had to be captured inside the lot.

Very early in the design process, Billy took another trip to Europe, to Vicenza, and to Paris. In the morning of the last day, he went to Notre Dame Cathedral. In the crossing there was some iron work, which appealed to Billy immensely; he thought it could be adapted for this job. After hours of hard work back in Middleburg, Billy succeeded making the adaptations. All the railings for the winding front stairs, the front balcony outside, the rear balcony, and the garden gate were based on what he saw at Notre Dame. It was erected by Noel Putman in The Plains, Virginia.

The owner's wife had been to college in California, where she had made Phi Beta Kappa; she had also studied at Oxford. During Billy's trip to Europe in which he had found the inspiration for the iron work, he looked up a great friend of hers, Madam Lepine, who showed him around Paris and also drove him to the historic spot of Veau-le-Viscount, France's most beautiful chateau, which was also the inspiration for the gardens at Versailles.

They also invited him to have dinner with them and another guest, Mrs. Stevenson from Cambridge University, the sister of the head of the Tate Gallery in London. Years later, Mrs. Stevenson gave Billy a dinner party in Cambridge.

Another family of enormous prestige lived near Middleburg, the Mills. Alice Mills, the daughter of a duPont, had built a house with a beautiful view, woodwork imported from England, and all sorts of stunning and unusual things inside. It was surrounded by a lovely garden, also very unusual. It had a swimming pool and needed a swim house. Mrs. Mills and her attractive daughter, Mimi, sat up late one night to design one. It was horseshoe shaped to fit the garden. Billy was called in to make it buildable, but her husband, Jimmy (formally a great polo player), had seen pictures of the Pan Am freight terminal in New York and thought the general shape of it would be just the thing. So once more, Billy had to draw it up. He took the sketches, not thinking they could possibly want to build it. However, the next time he went there, there it was, all built. With the unusual garden and plants around it, it didn't look bad at all.

Mrs. Mills was known for her great dinner parties. Once Tilly Loesch was invited. Billy was seated between her and Mrs. Mellon. She was so attractive that he could hardly spare the time to also talk to Mrs. Mellon. Another time he was seated by a beautiful young lady from England. She was so attractive that Billy could hardly stand it.

Finally, Mimi, the daughter, decided to come back from England and settle down in Middleburg. She had a most attractive house, which she was remodeling. One evening, she called Billy saying she wanted something, which she called a "breakfront" designed. Neither she nor Billy knew exactly what a "breakfront" was. However, Billy went out to inspect.

The room concerned was on the end of the house and was to be an "East Indian" room. She had had a nice young architect, a young woman, doing the work. However, her ideas were insufficient for the task. Billy decided the "breakfront" should go not where Mimi first suggested, but around the corner, facing the main room. As usual, there was a disagreement with her husband, Billy Able-Smith, an Eaton graduate who was said to be related to the Queen. The former architect had put in a line of stock windows, all glass, along the outside wall. Billy suggested column capitals and bases for all of them. The Architects Supply Co. in Chicago had just the things.

The "breakfront" was extremely difficult. It had to be exactly the right size and shape. It went between an exterior door and another opening, and had various important requirements inside. Due to the East Asian characteristics of the room, Billy decided that the panels must be painted with scenes of East India. He persuaded Mimi to employ her favorite artist, Wally Nall, to do the work. The results were extraordinary.

CHAPTER 23

Time passed, and Billy had long ago repaid all his debts. He had a good staff in his office. He had plenty of work for the future. He had a fine bank account. He was now a famous architect. He was a member of the Metropolitan Club, the City Tavern Club, the Laurentian Club, and the Middleburg Tennis Club. He had designed his own office, which was much admired. He had also made a beautiful plan for his own house.

He was content, except for one thing. He realized he had never really gotten over Mercer Jackson—his first real love who had affected him for years. That, combined with the Great Depression, had set him far back. He remembered Mercer, and several other women who had made him unhappy for a long time. This didn't seem right to him. If he had succeeded in marrying one of them, he might have lived a perfectly usual existence. Would this have been better?

Billy also wondered about his isolated beginnings. If he had not been born at Sweet Briar, had instead had an ordinary boyhood with plenty of friends, and grown up in and become accustomed to the great world outside the Sweet Briar gates, things might have been different. Billy's sister as a small child had been surrounded by other girls all younger than she and had received constant encouragement from their mother. When she graduated, she had received a medal for being the best girl in school. When Billy had graduated from prep school, there were no honors except a prize in French, which he only received because his teacher had met his sister and been so charmed that he raised his grade one point to let him get it. Billy was one of the few people in his class who had not been made a counselor until right at the end of his last year. All he had of his school years were difficult, tumultuous memories.

But despite a rough start, Billy had made the best of his talents. He had combined his artistic and academic prowess with a knack for social interplay. Billy had become an accomplished residential architect, running in heady Middleburg society, designing the finest homes. He did so for many years with great pleasure and satisfaction.

A young Billy Dew.

Billy at UVA.

The author's sister,
Polly Cary.

Billy's mother, Natalie Dew.

Even in his later years,
Billy piloted his plane.

The entrance to the author's Middleburg office.

Billy in costume on his
trans-Atlantic cruise.

The author in 1995, in front of the Middleburg
Community Center, which he designed.
(Photo courtesy of Howard O. Allen)

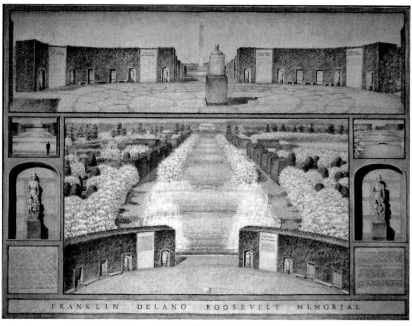

A photograph of Billy's submission for the
Franklin Delano Roosevelt Memorial competition.